BUILDING BLOCKS
For Strengthening Your Relationships

20 Philosophies To Strengthen and Build
The Quality of Love

by

Richard Flint

Learning To Face The Stumbling Blocks
That Weaken Your Relationships

Reprint 2005
Copyright 2002

ISBN# 0-937851-30-2

Printed in the United States of America.
For information write to
Flint, Inc.,
11835 Canon Blvd., Suite C-105,
Newport News, VA 23606-2570
or call 1-800-368-8255

www.RichardFlint.com

Cover Design by Denise Smith

Also by Richard Flint

Building Blocks *For Strengthening Your Life*

Building Blocks *For Strengthening Your Relationships*

Building Blocks *For Improving Customer Relationships*

Building Blocks *For Controlling Stress*

Breaking Free

Life Is A Maze

Quiet Please

Feelings

It Takes A Lot Of Pain To Grow Up

Reflections

Sometimes I Really Need To Cry

DEDICATION

*To those who have trusted me with
their life challenges. It's not easy to share,
but to those who have shared with me
this book is dedicated to their growth.*

TABLE OF CONTENTS

BUILDING BLOCKS
FOR STRENGTHENING YOUR RELATIONSHIPS

Building Block # 1:
A family is any unit of lives committed to a healthy direction.

Building Block # 2:
Love demands more than just being physically present.

Building Block # 3:
Life may not seem fair, but there is a lesson in every event.

Building Block # 4:
When you stop dating, you start drifting apart.

Building Block # 5:
Once trust is broken, it creates a permanent crack in the foundation of the relationship.

Building Block # 6:
Staying in love will be challenged by the times you fall out of love with each other.

Building Block # 7:
A child needs a parent, not a playmate.

Building Block # 8:
Let a child be a child as long as they are a child.

Building Block # 9:
If you can't work through the pain of yesterday, you can't create a better today.

Building Block # 10:
If you need a person more than you want them, you make them your personal slave.

Building Block # 11:
Marriage does not guarantee happiness.

Building Block # 12:
Love is an emotion you express, not something you buy.

Building Block # 13:
Avoidance doesn't resolve anything.

Building Block # 14:
It's not about changing each other; it is about learning to blend personalities.

Building Block # 15:
Couples that don't fight, don't grow.

Building Block # 16:
Issues don't create conflict; agendas do.

Building Block # 17:
Divorce doesn't end a relationship; it just changes the residences.

Building Block # 18:
Divorce punishes children when the adults forget their responsibility and act like children.

Building Block # 19:
"I love you" doesn't always mean, "I'm in love with you."

Building Block # 20:
If there is no time for you, you will soon resent what others ask you to do for them.

LAYING THE FOUNDATION
FOR THIS BOOK

How important is family to the foundation of our society? What part does family play in the moral fiber of our society?

How important is the home to the development of the lives that live under the roof? Does it really matter what happens behind the door where people share time and space?

How important are the relationships between husbands and wives, wives and husbands, parents and children, children and parents? Do those relationships affect how you see yourself? What happens to your life if these relationships are unhealthy?

It creates lots of questions about family, personal development and the relationships you share with those who make up the discovery parts of your life. These relationships create much of who you see yourself as, who you choose to fill your life with and the challenges your life will face as you strive to find yourself and learn how to fit others into your life.

The tragedy is — *many have become too busy to worry about these things.* The pace of their life is moving so fast it is a challenge for them to just keep their own life together. They don't have time to worry about others. The result has become an increase in divorces, children raising themselves, young adults fearful of relationships and a society with one of its cornerstones in a weak condition.

When I look back, I see a nation built on a solid foundation. I see cornerstones in place to make us stronger and protect us from the bombardment of concepts and ideologies designed to destroy us.

1

Today, those things we fought so hard to keep from destroying us are now the central issues that are weakening us from the inside out:

- *Divorce*
- *A Lack of Spirituality*
- *A Lack of Personal Accountability*
- *Moral Decay*

We all know that marriage at its easiest is challenging. "I do" is not a magical formula that guarantees you will live happily ever after. "I do" means *I will commit to my personal development and strive to bring the best of me to each day of this relationship.*

The challenge is too many say the words "I do," but have no idea what they mean. They think love will make all things good. Love is not a constant; it is something that is constantly challenged in the relationship. It requires daily effort. It requires all people sharing in the desire to grow together and build an environment that brings the warmth of happiness, the feeling of fulfillment and the sense of personal freedom. Yes, there will be trials; yes, there will be upside down days; yes, there will be times when emotions are stretched, but none of these are cancerous if they are recognized and confronted.

Most don't face issues. They find it easier to pretend they don't exist. That becomes an emotional trap, which at some point will raise its ugly head and collapse the foundation of the relationship. The result for most is divorce!

Interesting! People who are really "in" love with each other take the challenges they are handed and use them to make the relationship stronger. Their desire to have the relationship is stronger than the desire to throw it away. They understand they

2

and their mate are not perfect and imperfect people cannot have a perfect relationship. That means you don't run from your problems; you pause and address your concerns.

Communication can only happen when the challenges are faced as a concern you know has the potential to weaken the relationship. Addressing it now keeps it from being an emotional issue that can paralyze you later.

The only problems you will ever have are the concerns you didn't address and in not doing so allowed negative emotions to create your inner sight. The greater the emotions the harder it is to work through the situation. Store enough of these emotions and the weight of frustration becomes greater than the desire to move forward. The result is divorce.

There have been so many times couples have come to me for help and my wish was they had gotten to me sooner. There were so many stored negative feelings that their agenda has moved from working things out to hurting each other. The damage they had done had turned their love to hate. If only they had slowed their life down and addressed their concerns, rather than storing their feelings and reacting to their problems.

Divorce is simply the result of two people becoming strangers in their relationship. It doesn't have to happen, but most are too busy running from self to be able to focus on each other. The result has been a weakening of one of the most important foundations — marriage.

The weakening of our spirituality has created another point of weakening the foundation. What has happened to values? What has happened to our foundation of right and wrong?

We get upset with the way other cultures treat their people. We stand tall in our condemnation of their behavior, but

3

we don't hold ourself to the same set of standards. It is okay to lie and cheat, because we didn't kill anyone. It is okay to steal from others in order to have more for self, because we didn't kill anyone. After all, that's business!

The loss of a spiritual foundation can be seen in a society that makes excuses for its behavior. The loss of a spiritual foundation can be seen in people's irresponsible behavior. The loss of a spiritual foundation can be seen in greed that guides so many.

Many have rewritten the Golden Rule to read *do unto others before they have a chance to stick it to you.*

A person with a weakened spiritual foundation becomes a person who:
• doesn't hold others accountable for their behavior.
• is driven by greed, rather than their concern for people.
• create their own set of rules to justify their behavior.
• lack moral fiber.

When spiritual values diminish, society has no foundation of right and wrong. All decisions become opinions, not beliefs based on a set of guiding principles.

As much as many may see the Bible as an outdated history book, is has been and remains the most read spiritual guidebook of all times. The messages of life, love, truth and salvation transcend the corridors of time. It is the timeless message of God's love for people.

Our founding fathers understood the need for a strong spiritual foundation. They made "In God We Trust" one of their foundation statements. Today many seek to remove God from as many places as possible. We have moved from "In God We Trust" to "About God We Fuss."

No matter what your religious persuasion may be,

4

there is no way you can deny the need for a strong spiritual foundation. It is from this foundation your definition of right and wrong is created. It is from the spiritual foundation that you learn how to experience and give love. The spiritual foundation provides you with an inner guidance that goes beyond your limited sight.

Then, there is the cornerstone of accountability. This is a critical aspect of anything improving. If a society refuses to be held accountable for its behavior, there is only confusion. If people are not willing to be held accountable for their behavior, we live in a world where anything goes. Wrong is wrong and there should not be justification for it.

Look at our legal system. It is no longer about right and wrong. It is about wrong being made right. When a person commits a wrong and doesn't have to reap the consequences, there is nothing to restrain others from doing the same.

Look at our prisons. Rather than being an instrument of punishment, they have become a club atmosphere where those who have been found guilty have more rights than those they victimized.

What kind of a message are we sending when wrongs can become okay through our theories of justification? What is there to prevent people from doing the wrongs when they know there are ways to justify their behavior?

When I was on the church staff, I would work with young people who had committed crimes. It was always interesting studying the behavior of the parents. The kids did not have to worry. Mom and dad would bail them out. I remember talking with this one young man who had been arrested for shoplifting. He didn't need to do it. His parents had lots of money; it was just something he and his buddies did for fun.

I asked him, "Are you sorry for what you did?"

He looked at me with a smirk on his face, leaned his head back and laughed. "No! Why should I be sorry? It is no big deal. My dad will make everything okay."

Know what? His dad had the connections and everything was handled. That young man didn't learn anything, because he was not held accountable for his behavior.

Several years later, he took a car for a joy ride and ended up killing himself and three other young people. I wondered what would have happened if he had been held accountable for his previous behavior.

Accountability is such an important part of building a solid cornerstone for life. Without accountability, there is no reason to think about what you are doing. Without accountability, rules do not exist. Without accountability, there is no respect for life and what it means. As accountability has diminished, so have morals and ethical behavior.

When one knows they will be held accountable and there are consequences to what they do, they think before they act. This has to start in the home; it has to start in childhood. All this chatter about the negatives of spanking a child has done nothing but feed the behavioral breakdown of society.

I am not supporting beating a child, but I am a strong advocate of swatting their behinds when they do wrong which they have already been talked to about. If I test the rules and there are no consequences, what will keep me from doing it again? NOTHING! *But*, make it clear to me that there are consequences and I will be held accountable for my behavior, and I will think twice about what I am doing.

The key to accountability with children is consistency.

Children will test; children will push; children will challenge parents to see where the line is drawn. If parents say one thing and do another, children know they can break the rules without serious consequences. The result becomes they don't believe their parents when they speak, and they don't respect them as parents.

I wish you could have spent time with me listening to young people talk about their parents. Time and time again, I would hear "my parents don't care what I do. They are too busy with their own problems to be concerned about me."

I would hear "I wish they did care. I do these things to get their attention. It really doesn't matter what I do. Look, I am here and they didn't have time to come."

People need to know that rules are rules, not simply statements without consequences. The difference is accountability.

Put all these together and you get the final cornerstone that is decaying our moral fiber. Too many have become people without a conscience. When there is no strong family, when there is no spiritual foundation, when there is no accountability, there is no strong society.

When it is okay to lie, okay to steal, okay to cheat people, okay to use people to achieve your own greedy agenda, there is no longer a society with values.

Moral fiber is your inner foundation that keeps the ugly aspects of your personality locked away. When your ugly is loose, you are dangerous to yourself and all who are part of your life. When your ugly is loose, you have no reason to be good. After all, you can always find an excuse that others will accept to justify your behavior. Hey, you had temporary insanity. Therefore, you are not responsible for your behavior.

7

Say what you want, but 99% of the struggles we are facing today go back to the lack of a strong family environment.

As a nation, we have to get back to family. Everyone knows that, but few are doing anything to strengthen the family environment. We still make divorce the #1 option when there are family problems. We still have people marrying saying from the outset "if it doesn't work, we can just get divorced." We still have children in adult bodies having babies to hold their relationship together. We still have people who don't address the issues, because it is easier for them to avoid them.

Building Blocks For Strengthening Your Relationships is an honest look at twenty principles I have used in working with families. They are more than statements; they are foundational thoughts designed to help all aspects of relationships find solutions, rather than expand the confusion that will destroy all the people involved. No one walks out of a broken relationship a whole person. Yet, if you stay in an unhealthy relationship, you stay unhealthy. The challenge is to face what is really happening and create a solution path that becomes win-win for all people. These principles will help you focus on insights that can lead you toward a positive solution. They are not magical formulas; they are simply thoughts designed to slow you down emotionally, open you mentally, ask you some very honest questions and give you insights to make the right decision.

Life is not about the situations you are handed. It is about the questions you ask. All situations contain right and wrong questions. Ask the wrong questions and you feed your confusion and strengthen your frustrations. Ask the right questions and you find the solution and free yourself to move forward with positive energy. The direction is your choice.

Each day is either filled with Building Blocks or Stumbling Blocks. You choose which of the two you are working with.

FAMILY IS
*A family is any unit of lives committed
to a healthy direction.*

One thing is for sure; the look of the modern family has changed. What was once the traditional family design of mom, daddy and children has been redesigned.

Today in many situations there is the dual household with dual parents, hers, his and our children. Today there is the shuffling of children between households, which may be in different cities and different states.

The new look of the family has increased the tension between those who make up the picture. It has added stress trying to figure out who gets the children at what time and weakens the spirit of unity among the family members.

It is the weakening of the spirit that really concerns me. Family is about togetherness. It is about individuals coming together and sharing a common agenda of healthy growth. It is about lives growing up with a healthy view of who they are, where they are going and a sense of support they can depend on.

When the spirit of family is weakened, it takes away the calmness you need to feel secure in what is happening in your life.

Many weekends I have spent my time in the church environment doing a Family Life Conference. During the weekend, I would talk to parents about <u>The Meaning Of Being A Parent,</u> talk to teenagers about <u>Staying Calm With Your Parents When They Don't Understand You </u>and then my favorite session with children on <u>How To Raise Your Parents</u>.

11

Family is about the spirit of togetherness!

It is my belief good parents are not born; they are raised by their children. If you are a parent, you know how true this is. Your first child becomes your test. You don't know what you are doing and there really aren't any manuals. It would be great if when they are born, they came out with an instruction manual in their hand. They don't, so you are left to figure it out on your own. Oh, there are always those who will tell you what you should do, but it really is on the job training. So, the first one gets more attention than they need.

I guess many parents think they have this thing called raising children mastered, so they have a second one. The challenge is *that second one is not the same as the first one.* That child comes out and is a completely different personality than its sibling. Now, what do you do? You have to start all over again. The first thing you do is question your sanity. Why did you do this to yourself?

I guess the insanity is proven when they have a third one. Maybe they think after two they know what they are doing. What a rude awakening when the third one is not like the other two. Now, you have to start the parent-training thing all over again.

Each child teaches you something about yourself. Each child has the ability to emotionally turn you inside out. You really don't raise them; they raise you.

This is why I really enjoy the session with the little ones between the ages of 8 and 11. They are so open. They don't have any secrets and neither do you. Ask them a question and they are eager to answer it. I know enough about some parents to blackmail them. It is an exciting time of fun and discovery.

I had finished the Saturday morning program with a group of about 80 children and was sitting on the edge of the stage answering questions from a group. Out of the corner of my eye, I saw her. She was just standing there looking at me. I knew she had a question, but wasn't going to ask it in the group. Slowly the group moved away and I motioned her to come sit by me.

"What's your name?" Was my first question to her. Without looking at me she said, "Sarah."

"How old are you?"

"I'm eight," she said as she slowly moved her eyes to look at me.

The look in her eyes told me she was really struggling. She looked down for a few seconds and then looked at me and asked, "Can I ask you a question?"

"Sure you can. You can ask me anything you want."

There was this long silence. The tears were rolling down her cheeks. She wiped them away and said, "Do I have a family?"

I paused long enough for her to bring her eyes back to me. "What do you mean do you have a family?"

"My mommy and daddy are divorced and my friends say that means I don't have a family. Do I have a family?"

My heart leaped out to her. You could feel the emotions she was dealing with. Her eyes were now filled with tears that were streaming down her face.

"Yes, Yes you have a family. You have your mommy and your daddy. They may no longer live together, but you have a family. Your friends are just playing with you. You have a family."

I went to the Pastor of the church and asked about Sarah. She was an only child whose parents had recently divorced. The divorce had gotten ugly and her parents had

14

retreated to acting like two children trying to punish each other. I asked if it would be possible for me to talk to them. The Pastor told me he might be able to arrange it, but the emotions were still running high.

It happened I got to talk to both of them. When they entered, you could feel the emotional discord between them. I told them I was not there to talk to them about their problems, but a situation that had occurred with their daughter. The good news was they were both concerned about her well being. As I shared what Sarah had said to me, I could feel them both emotionally calm down and reconnect.

We spent a couple of hours talking about Sarah and what their divorce was doing to her. We worked out a plan that would take some of the confusion out of her life. Even if they couldn't live together, they still had a responsibility to provide her with a healthy home and a calm definition of life.

Family is a spirit of togetherness and that spirit must not be destroyed. Even if the adults cannot live together, the spirit of family must not be destroyed for the rest of the family.

A family is a unit of lives committed to a healthy direction. Even if the households are not the same, it doesn't mean there cannot be a common agenda of growth for all involved. Even if there are separate households, it doesn't mean the spirit of love, growth and commitment to those who make up the family has to be thrown away.

Just because two adults don't love each other any more doesn't mean they cannot still rally together around the love for their children. Just because two adults have chosen to no longer share a love relationship with each other doesn't mean they cannot still express a common love for the children.

I wish many of the adults who have decided they are

no longer in love with each other would remember that their children still need to feel the love from both of them. When they are put in the middle, they don't understand and too many times blame self for what has happened between the so-called adults.

You can live apart and maintain the spirit of love for those who make up the family unit. You may fall out of love with each other, but that doesn't mean you cannot share a common bond of love for the others in the relationship.

To punish children for what adults cannot work out is one of the cruelest forms of punishment. Maybe the so-called adults cannot get along, but children need to feel love, not the hatred or anger the adults have for each other.

Family is a spirit of togetherness. You don't have to share the same residence for that spirit to continue to live. This spirit is about wanting the best for each other. This spirit is about loving the members even if you are not in love with one of the participants. This spirit demands mature adults being aware of what their behavior is doing and saying to the little lives that don't understand why mommy and daddy aren't together.

Put them in the middle and they feel responsible. Put them in an emotional situation they aren't mature enough to handle and you scar them for the rest of their life. Put them in the middle of the adults personal war and they become the causalities that get wounded as the adults fight without being concerned about who is standing on the battlefield.

A family is any unit of lives committed to a healthy direction. It is lives sharing the spirit of love, concern and a desire for all the people to experience positive growth. This is only possible when the negative emotions are controlled and not allowed to be the driving force.

Here are some questions for you to answer *honestly*:
  • *How is the spirit of togetherness in your family?*
  • *Do the children feel the love and acceptance from both parents?*
  • *What could you do to strengthen the bond of love between the members?*

How Do You Protect The Spirit of Family?

S *share an agenda of love*
P *positive presence when together*
I *invest in getting beyond any anger*
R *refuse to blame anyone for what is*
I *inwardly sense the need for a calm presence*
T *talk all things completely through*

17

I'M HOME

*Love demands more than just being
physically present.*

How important is friendship in a relationship? Is it possible two people can marry, share the same house, the same bed, even have children and become strangers? You know the answer to that question is "YES!"

More times, more than people are willing to admit, couples get married and then start their journey toward becoming strangers.

Before I would ever do a couple's ceremony I would try to talk them out of getting married. I figured if I could put a doubt in their mind, they shouldn't be getting married.

Friendship and the growth of friendship in marriage is a critical aspect of the marriage lasting and growing. When two people stop working on friendship, they start working on becoming strangers. Once the process of becoming strangers starts, each develops behaviors to justify the weakening of the relationship.

It is so sad to see two people who once said they loved each other, lose the feelings that made each so special to each other. It is so tragic to watch lives that once shared special feelings develop behaviors that take those feelings away. The looks and feelings they shared become a part of their past, not their present.

It is so sad to watch lives come apart because two people were too busy to continue to share special moments together. That was not their intention when they got married, but it became the behavior that tore their relationship apart. It became the behavior that took away *togetherness* and replaced

19

The #1 thing a human wants to know… they matter.

it with *abandonment*.

Sam and Ellie had been married forever. At least that is how they described their relationship. It was one of those relationships that may have been made in heaven, but could not be endured on earth. It was beyond rocky; it was a constant tremor that registered at least nine on the Richter scale.

The first session I had with them exposed the real issue. Sam came because Ellie made him. He did not want to be there and made it very evident.

It didn't take long for Ellie to emotionally unravel. Tears were something she was used to in her relationship with Sam. He knew how to push her emotional buttons. I am not sure he wanted to hurt her; he was just a tired participant in what was barely a relationship.

She had been crying for about ten minutes when she looked at him and said to me with the tears streaming down her face, "I just don't understand him. I feel like I am a stranger sharing space with him."

The look Sam gave her was one of total disgust. He didn't say anything. He just got up from his chair and moved to the window. He stood there in silence, staring into the distance.

Ellie's emotional vault was open and she couldn't stop the words from gushing out. "I can't continue to live like this. I am a person and I want to be treated with respect. I am his wife and I want to feel important to his life. I want to know that he loves me."

Sam spun around, looked at her with this expression of anger, walked over, stood over her chair and said, "You don't know I love you! Woman, what do you expect from me? I come home every night, don't I? Isn't that enough?"

Clearly, for Ellie, it wasn't enough. She wanted more.

21

She wanted to hear those words *I love you*. She wanted Sam to be there when he was there.

Love is an emotion that demands more than just physically being there. It requires mental and emotional presence. Simply coming home and being there doesn't really say *I love you*. Yet, how many couples come home to silence, spend their evenings watching TV and go to bed like roommates, rather than husband and wife?

The challenge is building the friendship. The challenge is striving not to become bored with each other. Most relationships settle into routines and then the participants live each day to repeat the routines. That takes some of the spark out of being together. The routine starts shortly after they get married and develops into the behavioral pattern that moves them away from being friends and toward becoming roommates.

Then, children come along. Yes, children are a joy, *but* they also can become the escape. The needs of the child become the justification for not spending quality time together as friends. Do you have any idea how many times I have heard *when you are a parent, you don't have time for each other?*

That is more of a justification, than it is a reality. There is always time for the things you really want to do.

One night on the road, I was out to dinner when I became captivated by the folks at the table next to me. I have become so good at listening to other people's conversations.

It was their tenth wedding anniversary. He had worked to make it a special evening. It was her favorite restaurant. He was trying so hard to make this a special evening. He had one challenge — two children at the age where they didn't want to sit at the table. These kids were on the table, under the table, running around the table. Finally, she took the two children to the rest room. You could tell by the changed look on his face he was fit to be tied.

Not wanting to be nosey, I leaned over and asked, "Are you having fun?"

The look that shot back at me answered the question. He took a deep breath and said, "I wanted this to be such a special evening. I did everything I could do, but she won't go anywhere without the kids. Every time I plan time for us she has to bring the kids along."

There was a long pause followed by a look of disappointment. "I am beginning to believe she just doesn't want to be alone with me."

By this time, the others had returned and he continued with the evening he hadn't anticipated. I couldn't help but hurt for him. His disappointment and hurt were very evident.

Friendship is something you have to work on. It is not automatic. It takes energy; it takes time; it takes a desire to have time with each other. If you wait for the right time to be together, it will never happen. It has to be a desire that is stronger than the excuses. Finding time for each other is a way of telling the other person *you matter to me.*

I have taught for years the *#1 thing a human life wants to know is that they matter.* That cannot be communicated just with words. It has to have behaviors that define through action how much the person matters to your life.

Before most get married, they don't question whether they matter or not. There is plenty of attention; there is plenty of quality time together; there is communication; there is dating; there are moments that neither forgets.

Then, they get married and the hunt is over. Their world

changes; they are married and dating doesn't seem to have the same importance as it did before they said, "I do."

One thing I would remind couples before they got married was "don't stop dating just because you are married." I would see them after they had been married for a while, and I would ask them "are you still dating?" The look they gave each other would answer my question.

Why do other things become more important than spending quality time together? What changes the mindset you don't need to spend quality time together after you are married? Here is what I believe.

Once many get married, they relax with each other. They now have this piece of paper that says they are together. The strain is off and they can let their hair down.

The challenge most don't understand is being in love is not an automatic forever thing. Just because you are together doesn't mean you can stop dating each other. In fact dating after "I do" is more important than dating before "I do." Why? Because you have set a standard of attention and affection. If you stop because you are married, you question whether any of what was, was really real. When that sets in, the relationship loses some of the spark that made it appear magical.

Marriages are not made in heaven. They are designed by humans who come together to form a union of togetherness. As long as togetherness is present, the relationship is special. When togetherness turns to existing together, the relationship loses the glue that made each feel so special, so loved, so important. At that point, the negative questions create emotional moments that spiral into human collisions. This weakens the feeling of being loved, turns friends into strangers and causes many to seek others who make them feel special. All this could have been avoided by continuing to date, rather than just coming home.

Here are some questions for you to answer *honestly*:
- *Do you feel special in your relationship?*
- *Do you still date?*
- *Are you becoming strangers?*

How Do You Continue To Build The Friendship?
B *build through attention*
U *understand togetherness*
I *increase the communication*
L *leave quality time for each other*
D *don't stop dating*

THE FAIRNESS OF LIFE
*Life may not seem fair, but there is a lesson
in every event.*

It is a common thought — *Life isn't fair!*
I would hear it all the time in the counseling room. People
would come in with the question "Why?" and expect me to be
able to explain all of life's situations. I would hear things like:
- Why me? I didn't do anything to deserve this.
- Why has God picked me out to punish?
- Why does my life go through all the crap?
- Why did God allow this to happen? Why
  didn't He pick some of the evil people?

These are the toughest questions in life to deal with.
The "why" questions generally don't have a black and white
answer. They are generally the result of an emotional trauma
that doesn't seem to make sense.

You sit there and seek to explain to them *there is no
correct answer*, and they become even more confused.

Some of the "why" questions can be answered. When
you study the person's behavior, the result the person is battling
with is the consequence to their behavior.

I remember the first time I had to deal with an AIDS
patient. Mark came to me and he was devastated. He had just
been told he had AIDS and he couldn't understand how a
loving God would allow this to happen to him.

"This isn't fair!" Were his opening words. "I don't
deserve to have AIDS."

"Mark," I asked. "Did you understand about the
possibility of AIDS when you entered this relationship?"

A lesson can remove the emotion of blame.

"Yes," he replied in a tone that displayed anger. "I knew about AIDS, but I never thought it would happen to me."

"Did you and your partner discuss having protected sex?"

"Yes, but he didn't want that."

"Mark, you made a choice and with every choice there is a result. This is the result of the choice you made. God had nothing to do with it. You cannot blame God for what you did. There is only one way to see this. You chose and reaped the result."

That was not what he wanted to hear. He wanted to hear *yes Mark, life isn't fair and you got something you didn't deserve.*

Reality is — life is not always fair, but with each event there is a lesson. Most people never learn the lesson because they are too busy looking for someone to blame for the consequence to their behavior. They don't want to hear about choices, consequences and responsibility. They simply want to blame the unfairness of life for what has happened to them. It is such a challenge to get them to emotionally slow down and see the decision, the behavior and the result. To do that they would have to accept responsibility.

Hey, what do you think would happen if people would slow down and look for the lesson, rather than speeding up and looking for someone or something to blame? Do you think we would have a stronger society?

I was on a flight from Cleveland to Atlanta when I met Jerry. It was another one of those times when someone was placed in my life to hand me a story to share with others.

Our conversation started with golf. You mention the word and you have my attention. I had on my Masters jacket and it immediately caught his attention. From golf, we moved to life and that is where I got to know Jerry.

He finally got around to asking me, "What do you do?"

"I travel speaking at conventions."

"What do you talk about?"

"Well, I help people find the pathway through their confusion."

"Wow!" He said with a sudden look of pain in his eyes. "I could have really used you five months ago."

He paused, turned toward the window and I knew he was gathering himself. I waited for him to emotionally come back. It was apparent the story wasn't over yet.

"Five months ago we lost our little son. He was two months old and died from SIDS. I rocked him to sleep that night, kissed him good night and put him in his crib. Little did I know that would be our last time together."

There was another pause and another moment of staring out the window to emotionally regroup. I could feel the pain and the need to talk about it.

"At first I didn't want to face it. I was angry with God. How could He do that to us? He had given us that little life and then He took it. That is not a loving God. That was not a God I wanted to have anything to do with."

There was another pause. Only this time his expression relaxed and some of the pain disappeared out of his eyes.

"My wife and I have spent hours talking about our loss. Those two months with Jacob were special. The problem was I wasn't there for any of it. My life was my business. I knew I would have time with him when he got older. I thought at that age it didn't matter whether I was there or not. My wife was there and she was all he needed. Then, he was gone.

The son I didn't have time for was gone and I would never have time with him. God used that as a wake up call for me. My life was so far out of balance. My priorities were so messed up. I was a one-dimensional person — work. That was all I did."

There was a long pause as he finished part of the conversation in his head. "Know what?"

"Tell me."

"I know God had a purpose in loaning Jacob to us for that two months. I know I will never let work consume my life again. We are expecting another baby in six months and I will be there with him. I learned a lesson that is carved throughout my entire fiber. Believe me. I will be there with him and my wife."

It is interesting how a lesson removes the emotion of blame. Blame is only present when you are lost in the darkness of not wanting to be held accountable. When the lesson is present, awareness happens and you can see beyond the event.

The challenge is wanting to find the lesson. It is not always handed to you on a silver platter. You have to want to find it. Until you do, you are trapped in a world you have to blame in order to exist. Blame becomes the way you think you are holding it together. Reality is you cannot hold it together; you can only survive the moment and become less of a person in the process.

The lesson is always present; you may not be there seeking to find it. You have to slow down, examine your emotions, find a calm place to review what happened and open yourself to seeing the lesson. It is there waiting for you.

Here are some questions for you to answer *honestly*:

- *Do you think life has been unfair to you?*
- *Is there any anger hiding inside you?*
- *Do you see the power of lessons?*

How Do You Find The Lessons When Life Doesn't Seem Fair?

F *face the event with an open mind and spirit*
I *invest in a quality set of ears to listen*
N *never retreat into internal anger*
D *deal with your pain*

THE POWER OF DATING
When you stop dating, you start drifting apart.

He came to me when I finished my program and I could
tell he had something he needed to say. It didn't matter whether
I wanted to hear it or not; it was going to be said.

"Interesting thoughts you had about dating. I really
don't agree with the importance you place on going out. I date
my wife, but we stay home. She knows I care. We actually have
a date every night. We have dinner and then go into the living
room where we sit in our recliners and watch TV. Besides, this
dating stuff is expensive and I can't afford to take her out."

With those words, he had said all he had come to say.
He turned and walked off. The couple that was standing there
looked at me and said, "He didn't get it. He just didn't get it. I
bet his wife is one bored woman."

In an earlier chapter, we talked about friendship and
dating. I want to push this idea of dating a little deeper. Dating
is also an emotional journey that keeps you learning about
each other. It is more than just planning an evening out. It
is an opportunity to break the home routine and gather new
experiences. Those new experiences will keep breathing new
life into the relationship. Without that new life, the relationship
becomes trapped in sameness. Without fresh air blowing
through the relationship people become bored with what they
have.

Jerry came to me when his relationship with Sarah had
turned upside down. "I don't know what happened," were his
words.

"Richard, things seemed to be going so great and then it
just fell apart."

33

Boredom is the result of the lack of fresh air in the relationship.

"Jerry, tell me about a typical week in your lives."

"Well, we both work. Sarah's job has become a lot more demanding. I see her coming home drained. I guess we do what every couple does. We come home, have dinner, watch some TV and go to bed. Get up the next day and do it all over again."

"Do you help her with dinner or other things around the house?"

"Sometimes. Most evenings I have so much paper work to do I sit in front of the TV and do the paper work while she takes care of the house things."

He could tell by the look on my face I wasn't happy with what I was hearing. "Not good huh?"

"Jerry, when was the last time you took Sarah out on a date?"

"You mean like out to dinner and a movie?"

"Yes, that is exactly what I mean."

"Well, we were going to go out for Valentine's Day, but I got stuck at the office. I guess the last time we really went out on a date was about seven months ago."

Again, he could tell by the look on my face that was not a good thing.

"Jerry, do you think a marriage can get stuck in a rut?"

"Yes! I think that is part of what has happened to us. We are trapped in this routine that just keeps adding more stress to our lives."

"You're beginning to get the picture. Your life has become boring and Sarah has gotten bored with you. You are the only one who can change that. I want you to buy her some flowers, make a reservation at her favorite restaurant, take her out to dinner and apologize for being a big dummy. You have

35

been treating her like your housekeeper, not the woman you say you love. You haven't been making her feel special."

I paused to make sure he was still with me. "Jerry, all women want to be dated. Just because you are now married doesn't mean Sarah doesn't want you to still date her."

"But, she is always tired!"

"Tired of what? Think she might be tired of being treated like your housekeeper? Do you think she might be tired of watching you sit in front of the TV while she does house things? Do you think she might be tired of not feeling special in your life? You need to wake up and see what your behavior is saying to her. Jerry, you are treating her like a casual possession, not someone you love."

Jerry did what I asked him to do. Not just once, but now he and Sarah have a regularly scheduled date night each week. One week Jerry plans the evening and the next week Sarah plans what they are going to do. Neither knows what the other has planned until the morning of date night. I wish you could see them today. They are like two kids who have just met. Their relationship has become much healthier.

Dating is more than two people going out. It is a way of telling the other person *I still love you and am proud to be seen with you.*

There is a big need in relationships for affection. Affection is the attention you pay to that special person in public. Every person who loves another person wants to feel special to his or her mate. They want to go out and feel like the most important person in their life. When dating stops, affection diminishes. That takes away the feeling of being adored. You date someone you adore; you hide someone you just go home to.

36

Dating, also, strengthens the passion between two people. Passion is what you express when you are in private. Passion is what keeps romance from simply becoming sex. When sex is all couples have, it doesn't fulfill the desire to feel loved. When sex is all couples experience, it cheapens the experience and makes participants feel used. Over a period of time, that makes sex a turn off and romance a non-issue.

If you want to know the strength of passion and affection in a relationship watch a couple out to dinner. Does he open her car door? Does he open the restaurant door for her? Does he help her be seated at the table? Does he pay attention to her while they are dining? Does he participate in the conversation at dinner? How many times do the little intimate times stop happening after they are married?

One night on the road, I decided to venture out of the hotel to a nearby restaurant for dinner. Most times I just stay in the hotel and eat, but I wanted something different. As I was walking to the front door of the restaurant, this car pulled into the parking space by the door. The guy got out, started to the door when he noticed the lady he was with was still in the car waiting for him to open her door. He looked at her and motioned her to get out of the car. Well, you could tell by the way she closed the car door she was not happy. He walked to the restaurant door and proceeded to enter in front of her. The door closed just as she got there. She followed him in and as luck would have it, they were seated at the table next to me. I thought, "This is going to be an interesting evening."

He took the chair that was facing the TV in the bar. There was a basketball game on and you could tell the TV was of more interest to him than she was. She tried her best to talk to him, but all he did was watch the TV or follow the waitress

37

each time she walked by. It didn't take long and you could physically see the life sucked out of her by his behavior. Soon, she just settled into eating alone, even though he was there. You knew this was a relationship that was in trouble.

Dating should continue to add spark, energy and romance to the relationship. It is more than just going out. It is an evening that adds value to each person individually and to the couple together. It should be a time of renewal and reassurance. It should strengthen the relationship.

Dating should not be something you know you should do; it should be something you want to do. It should be a statement of love and commitment that builds trust and strengthens the resolve to build this into something that is just getting better and better.

Here are some questions for you to answer *honestly*:

- *Are you still in love with your spouse?*
- *Does your behavior make your spouse question your feelings about them?*
- *Are you affectionate as well as passionate?*

How Do You Continue Dating?

D *don't let the passion die*
A *agenda management - schedule dates*
T *take turns planning the date*
E *emotionally stay centered*

TRUST

*Once trust is broken, it creates a permanent crack in the
foundation of the relationship.*

Relationships are a puzzle that seems to keep
rearranging itself. The pieces of the puzzle reshape as the
relationship goes through its constant redesigning.
When two people are dating, the puzzle has one shape.
If they decide to live together before they get married, it has
another shape. When they get married, it takes on another
shape. When children arrive, there is another shape. As the
children grow and go through shaping their own puzzle,
the puzzle of the parents is reshaping itself. If and when the
children leave home, there is another shape. If there is a death
or a divorce, there is another shaping.

The greatest consistency of a relationship is the
reshaping. Each relationship is constantly reshaping itself.
These reshapings are emotional. You don't just walk up and
walk through. Each aspect of the reshaping is an emotional
experience. The better prepared each participant is the easier it
is to face and move through the transformation. The emotional
presence each brings is controlled by the strength of the
relationship. If the relationship is weak, each reshaping will
challenge commitment and resolve. It is at this point that many
exit. They don't want to have to wrestle with all they will have
to do to move the relationship to the next level. The price is too
great for them and this provides them with a reason to leave.

We talk about the glue that holds relationships together
during these times being love. Yet, love is a composition of
several different components. One of the most important is
trust.

Love is an emotion with several different components.

This is the element of love that allows one to control worry, doubt and the times of behavioral uncertainty. When trust weakens, the relationship goes through tremendous times of uncertainty. If the trust is broken, the relationship suffers a permanent crack in its foundation.

The most frequently asked question I get asked when talking about relationship is "if the trust is broken, can it be rebuilt?" The answer is "NO!" Trust is one of those components that has to be without any negative aspects. The second any negative aspect enters trust loses the solid foundation. When the solid foundation is not intact, cracks are created which contain negative emotions. These negative emotions invade what used to be a solid foundation and weaken it from the inside out.

Trust is about character. Your word is one of the most important points of integrity you have. In a relationship, your spoken word is what others accept with blind faith. They accept what you say and believe your behavior will stand behind it.

Trust is about respect. When you respect another person, you will not do anything you know if they found out about, would hurt them. If you can knowingly hurt them, you don't respect them.

Trust is about being in love with another person. When you are in love you want the relationship to get better and better. To do that you have to look at the other person from the inside out. You have to understand the need for you to improve in order for the relationship to grow. Each has to trust the other in doing their part; each has to believe the other is giving their best; each has to feel they are in this together. If this element of trust is not present, you will back away when you need to step forward.

41

I met Jeff while I was taking a few days off and playing golf in Florida. The first day out, we got paired together. It didn't take long for the small talk to turn to some inquisitive questions.

We were standing on the fifth tee box waiting to tee off when Jeff asked, "What are you doing here?"

"I needed a break from my schedule. I have been running so fast, I have run out of energy."

"What do you do?"

"I travel speaking to conventions."

"Any particular subject matter?"

"I deal with all those issues that confuse and frustrate your life."

Well, the look on his face told me I was an answer to some prayer he had prayed. "I'm here trying to figure out what to do. I just found out my wife has been having an affair with her personal trainer. It has been going on for almost a year and I didn't see it."

The tee box was open, so we teed off and made our way back to the cart. I didn't have to ask any questions. He needed to unload.

"I cannot believe I was so stupid that I didn't see it. I travel several days a week for business and never thought I had any reason to doubt her. I came home unexpectedly from a trip and caught them."

There was silence while he hit his next shot. "She told me it was my fault. If I didn't travel so much, I would have been there for her. I don't understand it. I have given her everything she has asked for. I let her design the house; she has the car she has always wanted; she goes shopping when and where she wants. I am never gone more than three days at a time. I make sure when I am home I help her with the children. I don't understand what happened."

He apologized for talking about it. "I'm sorry. I know you are here to relax and play golf. You are not here to listen to my problems. I just don't know what to do."

"Here are two questions I want you to think about. First, where is your love for her right now? Second, do you want this relationship? Don't try to answer them this moment, but think about them."

That was the end of the conversation for that morning. Later that evening I was having dinner in the restaurant and he came in. He spotted me, wandered over and I asked him to join me. I could tell by the look on his face something had happened since we had finished playing golf.

"You look like someone has emotionally beat you."

"I had a phone call from Tiffany. She said she was sorry and wants us to put all this behind us and move forward."

"How do you feel about that?"

"Part of me wants to pretend like it never happened, but a bigger part of me has lost trust in her. How do I know this is not just a ploy to get me back? We have a premarital agreement that states if she was ever unfaithful, she would get nothing in a divorce. How do I know this is not simply about her protecting herself? She sure wouldn't make it in the real world. I have spoiled her and she doesn't want to lose that."

"Okay, let's go back to my two questions for you. Where is your love for her right now? Do you *love* her or can you say you are *in love* with her?"

"I do love her, but I don't know if I can trust her. To be in love with someone you have to really be able to trust him or her. That is what I am struggling with. Can I ever trust her again?"

"What about my second question. Do you want this relationship? Is this something worth fighting for? Can you look at her and give her your total love and commitment?"

"At this time I don't know. I am just hurt. My emotions are all over the board. I want to be with her, yet I don't want to be around her. I want to hold her, yet I want to throw her across the room. I want to make love with her, yet I don't want to touch her. You're the counselor; would you say I am crazy?"

"Yes, you are crazy!"

The look on his face told me that was not what he was wanting to hear. When he saw me smile, he relaxed a little.

"There is no way you couldn't be crazy right now. Look at you. Your heart has been ripped out. The person you loved and you thought loved you has emotionally wounded you. How could you be a healthy person right now? It would be impossible."

"What do I do? Do I just pretend like it never happened?"

"Do you honestly think you could do that?"

"No! I know I cannot. I don't want to lose her, but I don't know whether I can trust her or not. Do you think it can ever be the way it was?"

"It is not important what I think. The important thing is what do you feel. This is not a mental thing; this is an emotional journey. You have to get your emotions together and determine what you really want here. You have to decide what it will take emotionally for you to get back into this relationship."

"I know it can never be the way it was. I really know that. I am just trying to fool myself. I guess I need to sit down

44

with her and really talk this through. It will be difficult. I don't know if I can do it without losing my temper. I have a big one and when it is loose, you had better stay out of my way."

Jeff stayed for two more days and each day as we played golf, we talked a little more about the emotions he was struggling with. He went back home and confronted the issue with her. Several weeks later I received an email from him informing that after talking with her, he didn't believe he could really trust her. Rather than facing the issue, she kept going back to blaming him. She didn't want to take any responsibility for what had happened. The last I heard from him they were working their way through a divorce.

How important is trust to the foundation of a relationship? How important is it the foundation not be cracked? Without trust, there is no solid foundation to build on. There are only moments to create doubt. Once doubt enters the relationship, it becomes driven by "what could happen," rather than "what we are going to achieve together." Once this pattern of behavior sets in, you open the door to all the other relatives that doubt brings to the negative party. Your emotions take over and you become a reactor, rather than someone who responds.

Here are some questions for you to answer *honestly*:

- *Is the trust in your relationship solid?*
- *Can you tell your spouse everything?*
- *How important do you think trust is?*

How Do You Protect Trust?

    T *talk things through*
    R *respect for each other*
    U *unravel all points of confusion*
    S *stay focused on growing the relationship*
    T *truth at all times*

FALLING OUT OF LOVE

Staying in love will be challenged by the times you fall out of love with each other.

If you turn me loose and let me speak about any topic I want, I will always talk about relationships. I don't think there are any subjects more important than dating, marriage and family. These are really about building relationships. All relationships are either healthy or unhealthy. There is no middle ground. The relationship is either growing or deteriorating. The tragedy is — *most are deteriorating.*

I was in Tampa, Florida doing a program on family. During the program, I made the statement, *all couples fall out of love with each other on an average of once every four to six years of marriage.*

It was fun watching the faces of people when I made that statement. Most people never consider the concept of falling out of love as a natural part of the relationship. Once they understand this, things that happen in the relationship that seem out of place start to make sense.

After the program, I noticed this couple had stayed and I knew they wanted to talk. I stopped packing up my stuff, sat down and motioned them to come join me. The look in their eyes said they wanted to talk, but were nervous about talking. Most who have that look walk away. They didn't!

They approached, hand in hand, looked at each other and then sat down. They were so nervous it was actually cute.

"I don't bite; I am not critical: I have a great set of ears. Let's talk."

That made them laugh and some of the tension was broken.

47

*All couples fall
out of love;
that is a given.*

Matt started with "Richard, we think we are at one of those crossroads where we are falling out of love with each other. We don't want this to be a negative. What can we do?" I watched as they squeezed each other's hand a little tighter and knew this was a very serious time for them.

"Amy, do you agree with what Matt has just said?"

She looked at Matt, looked down and then looked me squarely in the eyes. "Yes, I think we are at a very important time in our relationship. We have been married for five years. I know we love each other very much, but lately we have been at each other's throat. Things that normally wouldn't matter have become major issues. We fight about everything. That's not us. We have been so great about talking things through. We usually don't let things fester. We told each other when we got married we wouldn't be like our parents."

"Matt, tell me about your parents?"

"I grew up in a home where nothing was ever talked about. The tension between my parents was overwhelming. My dad used to talk to me about my mother. My mother would talk to me about my father. Neither talked to each other about what they were feeling. They just stored it and then beat each other mentally and emotionally. I think the only reason they stayed together was for the kids. We would have all been better off if they had just gotten a divorce."

"Amy, tell me about your parents?"

"My story is just like Matt's. Only, my parents got a divorce. That didn't stop the bickering. I would see my dad and he would chew my mom up and spit her out. At home my mom would always complain about my dad. I wanted to tell them both to *shut up!* After Matt and I got married I sat down with each of them and told them I wouldn't be around them if all they were going to do was beat the other one up."

There was a long pause. They sat there looking at each other tightly holding hands. I could tell they were fearful of this happening to them.

"Richard," Matt said, "We take what you said tonight very seriously. We think we may be going through one of those times when we are falling out of love."

"What makes you think that is happening?"

They looked at each other waiting for the other to say something. Finally, Amy looked at Matt and said, "We don't seem to be as close as we used to be. I mean we don't seem to enjoy each other as much. We don't do as much talking. Matt doesn't seem to help me with the things around the house he used to. I find myself upset with things he does. He has always done them and they didn't bother me. Now! Now, they seem to get under my skin."

Matt waited for Amy to take a breath and jumped in. "There is a lot of truth to what she is saying. I don't do as much as I used to. Not because I don't want to. I just thought she didn't appreciate what I did do. So, I decided to stop. And yes, things she does get to me. I never thought we would be here."

They were still holding hands and you could see the fear they were both experiencing.

"We don't want this to weaken our relationship. Richard, we love each other. We want to get through this without this tearing us apart."

They looked at each other and then at me. "Richard, do you think we can get through this?"

"YES! There is no doubt about you getting through this. You understand what is happening and the love you have for each other is strong. You just need to slow things down and make sure there is time for the two of you. The key is not avoiding each other, but making more special moments of together time."

A few months later, I received an email from them and things were going great. They had made it through the hurdle and came out on the other side stronger and with a deeper love. All couples fall out of love. That is a given. Not all couples recognize when they are falling out of love. Without this realization, their relationship gets weaker. How do you recognize when you are falling out of love with each other?

- *The disagreements increase.*
- *Little things become big issues.*
- *Communication decreases.*
- *Sexual desire weakens.*
- *Other things become more important than spending time together.*
- *A feeling of disappointment comes over you when you think about them.*

The key is recognizing when you are moving toward these crossroads in your relationship and being willing to slow down, rather than speed up.

You have to increase your personal awareness process. You have to sense when each is pulling away and call attention to what is happening. At this point, you have to slow down and talk about the emotions you are feeling. Falling out of love is not a mental process; it is an emotional experience. Your mind will work overtime to show you how to get through this, but your emotions are working just as hard to make you turn your back on what you are feeling.

You have to spend quality time together. Dating becomes more important than ever. You have to do the things

51

you enjoy doing together. You have to get out and rediscover how much fun you can have together.

You need to forget about sex and think only about romance. Dress to excite each other. Do things that make you remember why you fell in love. Do things that make you see how beautiful each other is. Touch and hold each other as much as possible. Recapture the romance and move away from just having sex.

Don't run from the fact this is happening. Face it head on and make sure both are willing to sit down and talk openly about the emotions they are wrestling with. Each must be prepared to listen without jumping in and trying to justify. Only by allowing each to express their emotions can you slow things down enough to really see what has lead to this crossroad.

Reality is *you will fall out of love with each other.* The truth is it doesn't have to weaken or destroy the relationship. If handled correctly, it can strengthen and take the relationship to the next level of love and romance.

Here are some questions for you to answer *honestly*:

- *Can you remember the last time you fell out of love with your partner?*
- *Are you there right now?*
- *Are you strong enough to face falling out of love?*

How Do You Recapture Love?
L *listen to what is happening*
O *open to changing your behavior*
V *variety is important*
E *emotionally reconnect*

WHO'S THE PARENT?
A child needs a parent, not a playmate.

Men and women can create a child, but not all who create a child can be a parent. This is such an important point. So many times in the counseling experience I have had a father or mother tell me, "I am their parent."

I have looked at several of them and said. "You could have fooled me. If you are this child's parent, why aren't you acting like it?"

Having a child is a responsibility. It demands more than giving birth; it requires adults who understand what they have done and are willing to accept the responsibility that goes with creating the child.

Too many have children only to wake up to what has happened. They didn't really think about what having a child meant. It requires making time for the child in your life; it requires being mature enough to handle the issues the child brings to your environment. It means putting aside some of your selfish agendas and have time, presence and patience for the life you have created.

A child is an investment of yourself in their development. They don't come with instruction manuals; they are not perfect creations; they will test and challenge you. *Yet,* they didn't ask to be born. That was a decision you made. Whether it was something you planned or not, it was a decision your behavior made.

With the decision came the greatest of all gifts — a human life. That life is special; that life needs help; that life needs hugs; that life needs direction; that life needs parents.

Parents are not born; they are created by children. The

Parents are not born; they are created by children.

child cannot define the quality of the parent they will have. Only those who are faced with being a parent can define the quality of what kind of parent they will be. What they must sense and accept is — *there is a life at stake here.*

Parents are the most important person in a child's development. What the child knows about life, love, emotions and about self will be taught to them by their parents. Most children's emotional issues can be traced back to their childhood. Most adults who find themselves wrestling with emotional issues are replaying the tapes they brought with them out of their childhood. It has to be clearly understood the importance of being a parent. There are human lives at stake here.

Peter was twelve when his parents brought him to see me. His parents had expressed concern over his behavior and wanted to know if I would help them find out what was happening.

When they entered my office, you could feel the tension. Mark, Peter's father, looked at his son and said to him, "I don't know what is wrong with this kid. There are days I just want to pick him up and shake him until he becomes a human."

There was a moment of silence where both Mark and Sally were looking at Peter. He didn't move. He just sat there looking into the distance. You could see the pain in his mother's eyes. It was evident she was the middle person between her son and her husband.

The silence was broken when Mark screamed at Peter, "What is wrong with you? Haven't we been good parents to you? I have given you everything you have wanted."

Peter turned quickly to his father and responded in a voice that was filled with fear and emotional uncertainty. "No you haven't. You may think you've given me everything I've wanted, but you haven't."

Mark was out of his chair and in the face of his son with his finger being thrust with anger. "What do you mean? What have you ever wanted I haven't given you?"

The tears were streaming down Peter's face as he moved back from his dad's emotional outbreak. "YOU! All I've ever wanted was you. You never have time for me."

Mark's face was red and the veins in his neck were puffed out. "I have given you things to show you how much I love you. I know I haven't always been there for you, but I have to work. You know my work requires a lot of time."

"I know," Peter said, "your work takes a lot, but that doesn't mean you can't spend time with me. I would give you back everything you have given me, if you would just spend time with me."

Peter's words caught his dad off guard. He stepped back, looked at his wife and then his son. His face was filled with first surprise and then a softer look as his eyes filled with tears. "I am so sorry son. I guess I have been going at this all wrong. I figured if I gave you things you would realize how much your mother and I love you and it would make up for the fact I couldn't be there."

He walked over to his son, knelt down in front of him, opened his arms and hugged Peter as he fell into his arms. "I am so sorry son. I never meant to hurt you. I love you. You are so important to me."

He looked at his wife and smiled. She was sitting there with tears streaming down her face. Mark reached over, took her hand and smiled. He looked back at his son. "Well Sally, I guess our son just taught me a lesson."

He looked at me with this big smile on his face. "Well, I think my son just taught me a big lesson in being a parent. I don't know how I got this so messed up. Thanks for helping us."

I smiled at all of them. I hadn't said a word. I just sat there and watched as Peter, the son, became the parent to Mark, his father. Mark never forgot that experience. He redesigned his life so there was time for Peter, time for him and Sally and time for the three of them. Peter has matured into a very healthy young man. Not long ago we all sat down and laughed about that day in my office.

Being a parent is a responsibility you accept when you choose to bring a child into this world. It is not something you can reverse. Being a parent is a lifetime commitment.

Becoming a parent is a real growth process. It is not something you are just because you have had a child. I have met those who have a child and become their playmate, rather than their parent. I have met those who have a child and disappear, even though they are there physically.

Becoming a parent is a growth process. A child is the most precious of gifts and deserves to have parents who are there as part of their life.

Being a parent means giving hugs. Children need to feel loved. Too many grow up not understanding the emotion of love. Their parents were not people who hugged. They didn't express physical love to the child. This leaves the child with an emotional void.

Hugs are an emotional way of saying *I love you.* It allows the child to feel the love, not just hear the words. Before the child is born, there is a special closeness with the mother. That feeling of closeness needs to be continued after the child is born. Hugs tell the child *I am here for you.*

Being a parent means understanding gentle firmness. There are many different presences that go with being a parent. Sometimes you laugh with them; other times you cry with them. There are times when their behavior means you have to discipline them.

The different presences required are not easy for many. The environment they grew up in will create which aspects of emotional presence they are most and least comfortable with. Reality is *you have to be able to be what the situation requires.*

There are times when you have to be strict. Children will test parents. Don't forget they have the best and the worst of each parent. They are smart enough to know how to use each part against each parent. They will figure you out long before you figure them out. It is challenging to be logical with someone who thinks like you. The key is to stay calm when you are having a conversation with a child who sounds like you. This is when parents must step up and present a common front.

Being a parent requires consistency. There must be a common front that tells the child *you cannot play us against each othe*r. There is none of this go *ask your mother or what did your father say.* There must be consistency between what is being said. Without this, there will be confusion and a huge sense of frustration.

Being a parent also requires adaptability. As the child grows, parents must be adaptable to the needs of the child. What was right when they were 3 may not be the correct design when they are 13. You must adapt the rules to the maturity of the child.

Being a parent is about letting them fail. I don't mean

letting them physically hurt themselves, but letting them experience the bumps and bruises of life. If you protect them from life, they will not know how to handle life. If you jump in and always rescue them, they will not become healthy adults. The challenge with many young people is they have grown up in a world that protected them from failing, rather than teaching them how to fail and get up. Failure is one of the great teachers in life; to deny a child the right to fail is to not prepare them for living.

Being a parent requires letting them go. They will always be your children, but they don't always need you to be their parent. At a point they need you to cross the emotional bridge and move from being their parent to being their close friend. That means letting them have their life. When they become adults, they don't need you as a constant in their life. They need you to be there with ears and support, but not always be there with the answer.

Becoming a parent is a growth process. It is something you have to learn as you grow in your parenting skills. It will test you; it will expose your fears; it will show you what you feel about you; it will define your ability to love; it will give you highs and take you to your knees. It is the largest responsibility you will ever take on.

Here are some questions for you to answer *honestly*:

- *Do you really enjoy being a parent?*
- *Do the two of you agree on what being a parent means?*
- *Does your child or children really know you love them?*

What Are The Characteristics of a Great Parent?
P *patience*
A *adaptable when necessary*
R *responsive, not reactive*
E *emotionally sound*
N *not judgemental*
T *to know when to let go*

CHILDHOOD
Let a child be a child as long as they are a child.

The look on her face when she entered my office told me she was on a mission. She walked in, sat down, looked at me with a look of disgust on her face and said, "I need your help with Katie."

Katie was her eight-year-old daughter. A fun loving child who was everyone's best friend.

I paused, studied her facial expressions and responded very gently. "Sue, what seems to be the issue with Katie that has you so concerned?"

She leaned in and answered my question with these words. "She is not dating yet. There must be something socially wrong with her."

I wish I had had a camera to record the look that must have been on my face. I know what I was feeling on the inside. I knew I had to stay calm, but this was one of those times when you want to leap out of your chair and scream, "What is wrong with you. The child is only eight! Are you crazy or just stupid?"

However, being a trained professional you pause, get your wits back and respond. "Sue, you are concerned because Katie isn't dating yet? She is only eight. What's the hurry with her dating?"

The look on Sue's face told me she didn't appreciate me questioning her about Katie. She leaned in and said, "If she doesn't start dating soon, her personality is going to be destroyed. She is going to think she is not desirable."

"Sue, do you hear what you are saying? You are using a sexual term to describe an eight-year-old child. She is just

61

Childhood is where children learn how to become a healthy adult.

a child. You need to let her be a child as long as she can be a child! Don't take that away from her."

That was not what Sue wanted to hear. "I can tell you are not going to help me. I thought you would understand this." With that, she got up and left my office.

Can you believe that? A mother worried because her eight-year-old daughter is not dating yet. The tragedy is — *that story is repeated in many different forms every day.*

Childhood is such an important time in the development of a life. It is where you learn how to smile, learn how to laugh, learn how to cry. It is where you learn how to be you. It is not a time that just ends. It is a growth process that continues throughout your entire life. When you lose your ability to be a child, you get old.

There are too many children today who are a child in age, but are old in spirit. They are not being allowed to be a child. Their parents need for them to grow up so they will stop being an intrusion in their life. Their parents need to live their life through them. That means *get over being a child.*

I met Gary and his son Matt on the golf course. I had the afternoon off and decided to get in at least nine holes. Since I was a single, they paired me with them.

"Hi!, I'm Gary and this is my son Matt."

"I'm Richard. Thanks for letting me tag along with you."

Matt walked over shook my hand and we began an interesting round of golf.

"Gary, how old is Matt?"

"He's ten and is going to be a professional golfer."

I laughed and asked, "Does Matt know that?"

The look on his face told me this was not a joking

situation. "I started him playing when he was three. He is a natural and I know he can one day play the tour."

I watched Matt play and you could tell this was not his first love. His behavior said he was here because dad made him.

During the round, it came out that Gary had always wanted to be a professional golfer, but didn't have the talent to make the tour. He tried, but didn't make it. If he couldn't, his son would! It didn't matter what his son wanted. He was going to be a professional golfer.

There are too many Sues and Garys out there. They are seeking to live the life of their child. After all, they are the parent and know what is best for their child. The reality is the Sues and Garys of the world are turning their children into psychological cripples. They are dysfunctional when it comes to living. They lack the emotional development that comes with being a child. They are unhappy with what they think life is and very angry without knowing why.

Childhood is where children learn how to become adults. If they don't have a healthy childhood, they don't become healthy adults. Let them be a child as long as they are a child. Don't push them by the most important time in their life.

I think there are certain parental behaviors that are having a negative affect on children. You don't have to agree with my observations, but in my working with children and families, I find these to be the largest negative contributors.

First, is the fact many are being forced to grow up too early. Like the lady and her eight-year-old daughter, many parents are seeking to live their life through their child. Yes, most children are more intellectual, but that doesn't mean they understand how to use what they know. Yes, they are maturing physically a lot sooner, but their bodies become their enemy. Everywhere they turn, they are having sex thrown at them. It creates questions most parents are not comfortable in answering. This means they are left to discover sexuality on their own. In the past few years, I have dealt with many sexually active eight, nine and ten year olds. They don't understand what sex really is, but they are inquisitive. The lack of a relationship with their parents opens them to exploring on their own. The fact many of their parents have pushed them to "act like an adult" has opened them to the sexual experiences.

Hey, let them "act like the child they are." Let them be a child as long as they can. They need all the childhood possible.

Second, is little league sports. The issue here is not the children. The issue is the healthiness of the environment. The environment provides them with a place where they can learn social skills, get healthy exercise and learn to be part of a team environment.

The challenge comes with the parents who are sending a negative message about winning and losing. The negative lesson comes when they don't allow the child to gain a healthy definition of failure. Winning becomes the only thing that matters. To these immature parents failure is unacceptable. Most of the time, these are parents who didn't excel in sports when they were a child and are living through their child.

Failure is one of the most important lessons any human can learn. Failure is not a negative; it is a step in learning how to succeed. If one doesn't have a healthy view of failure, they will not understand what real success is about.

Failure teaches a person resilience. It teaches you *life will knock you down, but you can get up stronger.* But, if one is taught "you don't want to fail" and they are not sure whether they can or not, what will they do? They will avoid failure — *which is not healthy.* They will make excuses — *which is not healthy.* They will spend more time staring at what they can't do — *which is not healthy.*

Failure is really about learning how to succeed. Until it is okay for one to fail, their life will be filled with never completing events. The result will be a life that doesn't understand what it can and cannot do.

Third, is the missing of grandparents from the lives of children. Grandparents are a very special part of any child's growth. Their role is to love them, spoil them, spend time with them and then, give them back to the parents. Every piece of research I have read tells me *children who grow up with grandparents in their life have a healthier definition of love and life.*

Our mobile society has taken many grandparents out of the life of their grandkids. An effort needs to be made to let the grandkids spend quality time with the grandparents.

Fourth, is unsupervised television watching. The TV has become a common baby-sitter. Kids are told to "go watch TV." The challenge with TV is what is on the screen. TV is not the most wholesome media today. It presents more negative, than it does positive.

Right along with this is the number of hours kids are spending playing computer games today. Many come home and go right to their computer. They spend hours either on chat lines or playing games. They do not play with their friends; their social skills are not being developed. They are becoming lost in a world of screens that are feeding their minds. Most of what they are mentally dieting on is not healthy for their

66

emotional makeup.

The last of these unhealthy factors facing children today is the rising rate of divorce. Divorce doesn't end a relationship; it just changes the residences. The number of children with three and four parents is mind-boggling.

We are going to talk about this one in-depth in a later chapter. Just know too many children get emotionally punished when a divorce happens and the parents become unruly children fighting to be right in a situation where both have been wrong.

Childhood is one of the most important aspects of personal development. Let a child be a child as long as they can. Don't push them; don't rush them; don't force them to become what they are not ready to be. Let them be a child.

Here are some questions for you to answer *honestly*:

- *Do you really understand the value of childhood?*
- *Are you a parent who pushes their child to grow up too soon?*
- *Did you have a healthy childhood?*

What Is a Child?
C *creation that is a gift*
H *handful at times*
I *investment*
L *lesson center for parents*
D *decision you chose*

THAT HURTS

If you can't work through the pain of yesterday,
you can't create a better today.

The most consistent thing about life is it will be filled
with challenges. There is no such thing as the perfect life. To
have the perfect life requires perfect people. Since your name
is not God, you will be faced with challenges that will test
your commitment and expose your fears. Since most are not
into learning from life's experiences, they get to repeat life's
situations they didn't learn from while they were going through
them. That means their life will lack positive consistency,
forward movement and the growth necessary to improve. That
means they live in the Circle of Sameness.

There are few things more exhausting than the Circle
of Sameness. It is like living the movie "Ground Hog Day."
You get up, face your day and find yourself repeating the day
you had yesterday. That sameness will wear you down; that
sameness will steal your creativity; that sameness will cause
you to react, rather than respond to what is happening in your
life.

The key to breaking free of the Circle of Sameness is
finding the lesson contained in the situation you are dealing
with. It is the lesson that allows you to exit; without the lesson
you are trapped and forced to repeat the situation all over
again. This is why you find so many people who are worn out,
tired of trying and angry with how their life is going.

The tragedy is — *this is the majority of people.* Their
life becomes a repetitive circle they can't see themselves
breaking out of.

I met Karla and Barry at my StarMaker Conference.

*Life is really not
about what you have been through,
but how you have faced the
challenges you have been handed.*

Her boss had paid for the entire staff and their spouses or significant others to attend. Karla and Barry had both been married before, had terrible marriages and were both deeply scarred. It was apparent they were in love with each other, *but* hurt from the previous relationships was so great, neither wanted to risk getting hurt again.

Karla had children still at home while Barry's children were grown. Barry's children would challenge their dad with "what is wrong with you? You are never going to find a woman better than Karla. You are going to fool around and lose her. Is that what you want?"

That was not what Barry wanted, but at the same time he didn't want to have another woman hurt him like his ex-wife. She decided she didn't love him or the kids and just left. Barry was left with two little ones to raise. His career was demanding, time was a challenge and he really didn't know how to be both parents. He met Karla and she gave him a lot of support. That was about all she could give.

Her life was not much better than his. Her ex-husband loved the bottle more than his family. He kept promising he would clean up his life, but his words were an empty well. Finally, Karla had had it and packed herself and the kids and left. She was a single mom working to raise her kids and provide them a good life.

The two of them were so cute together. You couldn't be around them without feeling the love they had for each other, *but* since they had not faced the hurt from their previous relationships, they wouldn't talk about getting married.

I sat with them one night and it provided an opportunity to talk about their past pain. At first they were not comfortable, but soon they were both very open about the emotions they were wrestling with.

I looked at them and asked, "When are the two of you going to get married? You have to plan the date, so I can put it on my calendar. I want to be there to make sure you both show up."

They laughed and then looked at each other. "We have sort of talked about it," Karla said. "We just don't want to rush into it."

"Rush into it! How long have the two of you been seeing each other?"

They looked at each other, smiled and Barry said, "Oh, I guess long enough to be beyond all this stuff."

He paused, looked at Karla and continued. "We both have so much baggage. It is as if we don't want to drag it into each other's life, unpack and end up like we did in past relationships."

"Karla," I asked. "Is Barry like your ex?"

"No! He is nothing like my ex."

"Barry," I asked. "Is Karla like your ex?"

"No! She is nothing like her."

"Then help me understand what is going on here. Neither of you are like the people you were married to, but each of you is fearful of being hurt again. Is that what I am hearing?

They looked at each other and nodded to me. "Isn't that just an excuse? What are you both afraid of? It is apparent to everyone who knows the two of you that you are in love with each other. It is apparent from watching the two of you together you enjoy each other's company. It is easy to see you have fun together. So, what's the big deal?"

Karla spoke first. "I know how much he was hurt and I

don't want him to go through that again. I don't know for sure whether I would hurt him. I don't know if I am beyond the pain of my past."

"Karla, have you grown since your divorce? Are you a different person today?"

"Yes, I have grown. Yes, I am a better person."

"Then, let go of what was. If that is all you can see, that is all you will be."

I paused long enough to let that soak in and then turned my attention to Barry. "Is your story like hers?"

"Yes, yes it is. I have a lot of resentment toward my ex. There are days when I hate her more than anything. When that happens, I am not a person you want to be around. I get down right ugly. That would not be fair to Karla. She deserves better than that."

"Barry, can you see your life without Karla?"

"No, and I don't want that to happen."

"Karla, can you see your life without Barry?"

"No, but I don't want to hurt him and I don't want to be hurt again."

"You are both hanging on to what yesterday was and in the process throwing away moments of special together time. If you can't work through the pain of yesterday, you can't have a better today. You have to be willing to take a risk. There are so few people you can blend with. Don't throw something meaningful and special to both of you away."

Today they are married and continuing to work on not letting yesterday become today.

Life is really not about what you have been through; it is about how you have faced the challenges your life has been handed. If you face them and find the lessons, you get to move beyond the emotions that have created your painful hurt. If you don't face the issue and find the lesson, you will continue to relive the painful hurt and become a person who is guided by the negative fear that unresolved pain creates.

Don't forget. *The things you think you are running from you are actually running toward.* The key is facing the issue, finding the lesson and implementing it. The lesson can only be found when you slow your emotions and allow your mind to become your growth partner. When you can find what the event has taught you and understand what it will take to not repeat it, you have found the lesson. That will demand patience, pace, truth, openness and desire that is stronger than your fear. The battle you are fighting is between your desire and your fear. The winner gets to plan your life.

Here are some questions for you to answer *honestly*:

- *Do you have any unresolved pain in your life?*

- *Do you find yourself thinking about the wrongs of yesterday?*

- *Does hanging onto pain hurt your life and your relationships?*

How Do You Move Beyond Pain?
P *pause and see the entire picture*
A *address the reason the pain is so hurtful*
I *interact with the right people*
N *never make it your only focus*

74

SLAVERY

If you need a person more than you want them, you make them your personal slave.

Karen was such a surprise to my life. I wasn't looking for her when she entered my life. She has told me "a man was the last thing she was looking for at that time in her life."

It is amazing how life happens. Twice before I had been close to getting married, but each time the lady had asked me to give up my career. They didn't want me to be gone as much as I was gone. The reality was they *needed* me in their life. Their "need" to have me in their life was much greater than their "wanting" me in their life. Therein laid the complication.

Karen was different. She was (and still is) very independent. She enjoys her time by herself. It gives her time to do the things she enjoys doing that I don't get a thrill out of. For many couples I have known that would not be okay. But for Karen it is.

How much fun can two people have when one is tagging along because they "had" to go? How can their together time be exciting when one doesn't want to be part of the experience? All that creates is pressure that fills the air while the two are there for "fun!" All it does is suck the enjoyment out of the event. When the event is over, they are both filled with disappointment. Since most don't talk about their disappointments, it just gets stored in their emotional vault of unresolved issues.

Couples should not do everything together. They each need some activities they do without their spouse. Couples can spend too much time together. When they cannot be apart, it is not a sign of how much they love each other, but

75

*Needing someone is not
as much about love
as it is about slavery.*

of a relationship that is based on a sense of "need" that is stronger than the desire of "want." The result is a relationship that makes each a slave to the needs of the other. That is not healthy, nor is it a relationship that grows in the depth of its love. It becomes a relationship that becomes filled with resentment and a feeling that neither has a life.

When Karen and I started talking seriously about getting married, I knew I had to explain to her where she would fit in my life. I had done enough work with couples that I knew the idea of *your spouse being #1 in your life.* I knew that would not happen with us and we needed to talk about it.

We were at dinner when the conversation happened. I am a firm believer that in relationships when serious discussions need to happen, have them outside the house. The house has too many emotions already stored in the walls. A neutral ground will remove some of the emotions and allow all to have a calmer presence. When too many emotions get tangled up in what is being said, there is no communication. There is just a space where the emotions shut the door to understanding.

"Karen, you and I need to discuss how you are going to fit into my life."

The look on her face told me she didn't understand what I was saying.

"When many people get married, they expect the other person to make them #1 in their life. If they don't get that position, they feel they are not really loved. I don't believe that is true. Being #1 in someone's life can be a statement that is denied through behavior. Being #1 in someone's life can also be a dangerous position. It can mean they *need* you there. It is important for you to understand I don't *need* you in my life; I *want* you in my life."

"I know that," she said. "You have been on your own for years and you don't *need* me to take care of you. I don't need you in my life either. I was doing just fine on my own. I still don't understand how all this happened. I wasn't looking for a man and then there you were. Don't get me wrong. I am glad you are here, but I sure wasn't looking for you."

"I know that. That is what makes this so special. I wasn't looking for you either, but when you appeared in my life, I couldn't get you out of my mind. I didn't understand why you appeared, but I am sure glad you did and then didn't disappear. I have had women appear in my life, catch my attention and then disappear. You didn't and that is how I know this is right."

There was this smile on her face. "I know what you are saying."

"Karen, what I do need for you to understand is you will never be #1 in my life. I cannot put you there. If I do, I will abuse the love we have and it will never really grow. *But*, I will promise you will always be #3 in my life."

I paused to make sure she was with me. I knew she didn't fully understand what I was saying.

"You see," I continued, "My #1 relationship is with God. That is where I draw my strength. My relationship with God is my source of calmness, clarity and confidence. God is my inner source that grants me understanding to what is and will be in my life. #2 is my relationship with me. I have to have a healthy relationship with me in order to have a healthy relationship with you. If I am not mentally and emotionally healthy, you and I cannot have a healthy relationship. If I am not mentally and emotionally healthy, I will constantly do two unhealthy things to you. First, I will blame you for what is wrong. I may not say it to you, but I will blame you for the wrong in my life. Second, I will need you to take care of me. That will make me dependent on you and you frustrated with me. I don't want that! I have seen too many relationships come apart because the *need* was much greater than the *want*. That only punishes the people and drives them apart."

That conversation set the foundation for our relationship. We have revisited it several times just to make sure we were still on the same page. I don't need Karen to take care of me. Yes, I enjoy the things she does for me. I can enjoy them because I know she does them out of love and not because she feels she *has to do them out of a sense of need*.

Do you sense the difference between *need* and *want*? If you need someone in your life, they are there to take care of you. They are there to fill a void that isn't being filled. Their value is in their meeting your need and filling the void. As long as they are doing that, you love them. If the need is not being filled, you question whether they love you. In this relationship the definition of love is based on them taking care of you.

That is not love! That is a form of slavery. They are there as your slave to take care of your wishes. Their value is in them taking care of you, not in them sharing your life with you.

If you *want* someone in your life, it is a different picture. If you want someone in your life, you have bypassed needing them to take care of you. Wanting someone is about sharing life with them, not needing them to do for you. Wanting someone is about respecting them as an individual, not seeing them as a possession. Wanting someone in your life is about enjoying their presence, not expecting them to be there for you. Wanting someone in your life is about building a partnership of togetherness, not a relationship based on one taking care of the other.

In a relationship based on *need* you really don't know the other person. Your picture of them is based on what you *need* for them to do for you. You don't experience who they really are. You define their presence in your life on what they will or will not do for you. That is not love! That is abusing what they feel for you. Over a period of time, they will grow to resent what you need for them to do and hate the fact they do it. That will destroy what they have felt for you and put a wall in place that keeps them from *wanting* you in their life.

To really know a person you have to *want* them in your life. That is the only way they will have the freedom in your life to be who they really are. When you want them in your life, you turn them loose; you don't hang on to them. When you *want* them in your life, you grant them passage in your entire life; you don't shove them in a corner and keep them there.

The tragedy is — *most relationships are based on need, not want.* This is one of the major contributors to the dysfunctionality of most relationships. The expectations are not based on the love for each other; they are based on the need to be taken care of. There is no growth in that formula. There is only the development of resentment, which will suck the life out of whatever love there may have been.

This level of dependency will destroy the real meaning of love. It will leave each with an unhealthy understanding of having someone in their life. If they are parents, it will convey an unhealthy definition of love to their children. It will send a message that weakens the strengths of love and set the life up for major disappointments. I would suggest to you this is what has happened over the years and is a major reason for the increase in the divorce rate. Many don't marry because they are *in love*; they marry because they have found someone who will take care of them. Then, when they stop taking care of them, the relationship is over. Why? Because they don't love them anymore.

Here are some questions for you to answer *honestly*:

- *Is your need or want stronger for that special person in your life?*
- *Are your expectations for each other unrealistic?*
- *Why do you love them?*

How Do You Build The Want and Weaken The Need?
B *believe in yourself*
U *understand their presence in your life*
I *invest in setting them free to be their best*
L *love them for who they are, not as a slave*
D *don't make them responsible for your happiness*

THE ILLUSION OF HAPPINESS
Marriage does not guarantee happiness.

Do you believe in fairy tale relationships? You know the ones I am talking about. Two people meet; it is love at first sight; they marry and live happily ever after. How many of those have you seen?

Some people believe when they get married, it guarantees happiness. It doesn't take long for the disappointment to set in. Just because two people say "I love you" and get married doesn't mean that happiness is going to be there forever and ever. For some it is not there when they say, "I do."

Mack attended a seminar I was doing for the Sales and Marketing Executives International. He really didn't want to be there, but one of his buddies said, "You have to go hear this guy. He will challenge you, make you think, get under your skin and become a constant force in your life."

As Mack put it later, "I didn't believe anyone could do that to me. I went just to prove to my friend he was wrong. I felt I really didn't need anyone talking to me about my life. I had convinced myself I was in pretty good shape. Wow! Did that three hours prove me wrong."

After the program, his friend introduced me to him with these words. "Richard, he needs your help. His life is upside down and he can't admit it. He lives in an imaginary world. He keeps telling himself he is okay. The truth is he is not okay and he is slowly emotionally dying."

The look on Mack's face said he was not comfortable with this conversation. He looked at his friend and his eyes said "I would like to kill him right now."

You bring to the marriage who you are, not who you want to be.

We visited for a few minutes and I told Mack, "If you need to talk, here is my email address."

He took it, looked at it and put it in his pocket. I knew he had no intention of contacting me, *but* I knew he would. You could tell from his presence his friend's words about his life were correct.

It was about three months later when I received my first email from him. It was about what was happening in his business, but you could tell it was just a test to see if I would really answer his email. I took his email apart and responded to each of his questions.

Within a day, I had a response back from him and this time it went a little deeper into his life. This time he opened the door to his marriage. The words he chose to describe his marriage gave me a picture of a relationship coming apart. I could feel his pain through the words he wrote.

I responded with one question. "Mack, are you happy in your relationship?"

I will never forget the response I got back from him. It started with "I don't think I have ever been happy in this marriage."

Those were interesting words. As I read the email, I knew he and I needed to talk. It happened my schedule allowed us to connect and have a few hours together face-to-face.

"Mack," I said. "I found your last email to be really interesting. Is it true you feel you have never been happy in your relationship?"

"Yes! I have thought about it for years. I should have never gotten married. I knew it was wrong. On our wedding day I knew I should call it off, *but* I didn't want to disappoint all the people."

He paused, looked at me with eyes filled with pain and continued. "The truth is I didn't want to face my mother. She had really been the one to arrange this marriage. She knew that Paula was the one for me. She pushed and pushed until I gave in to her pressure. If I had not gone through with the wedding, she would have killed me."

"Did you ever try to talk to her about how you felt?"

"Several times I went to her with the intent of explaining to her how I felt. Each time she would talk to me about how happy she was that Paula and I were getting married. That stopped me dead in my tracks."

"You and Paula have been married for almost twenty-seven years. You have four children. In that time have you ever been happy?"

"Richard, I don't think so. Each time I look at her, I feel empty. I have wanted to leave, but I would think about the kids and know I couldn't do that to them. Now, they are grown and on their own and I cannot use that as the reason to stay. I still look at her and know I don't love her. I know I am not happy and I can feel the life being drained out of me. I want to have a life and be happy."

"What does that mean?"

"I really thought if I hung in there long enough, happiness would come. I thought if I really try, I could make it through my feelings and fall in love with her. I have tried, but the happiness and the love haven't happened."

"Do you think Paula knows how you feel?"

"I have never hidden my feelings from her. I have told her I wasn't happy; I have told her I wasn't in love with her. She just looks at me with a look that says *he is just going through one of his moods.* After almost twenty-seven years she should know this is not a mood."

"What do you feel you need to do?"

"Part of me believes I need to move out, get a divorce and go forward with my life. Another part of me knows if I do, I will be tarred and feathered by lots of people. Our pastor will tell me I am going to hell; all my wife's friends at church will crucify me; my kids will not support me. I would probably have to move from here. That wouldn't be all that bad, but I don't know where I would go."

The pause told me he was thinking. This was a time for me to be quiet and let him process his thoughts.

"Then, there is the financial part of this. She has me so in debt it will take me forever to get out. I have talked to her about her spending habits, but she just continues to spend and spend. I will have to have money for the bills, for the house and for her. I don't make that much. I feel so trapped! I just want to be happy."

There are more than a few Macks out there. They are trapped. They are tired; they are frustrated with their life; they are slowly emotionally wasting away. They are not happy; they are an empty shell existing in a body that is just getting more and more tired. They don't have a life; they have an existence.

Marriage does not guarantee happiness. When you get married expecting the marriage to bring you happiness, it doesn't take long to realize the illusion of it all.

If you are not happy before you get married, marriage is not going to create a life where you just live happily ever after. Granted, it may create a period of joy, but that will go away as soon as you realize marriage is not a constant state of bliss.

For marriage to be filled with happiness it must involve two people who are happy with who they are. When marriage occurs and each person is expecting the other person to make them happy, they are in for an emotional collision. You bring to the marriage who you are, not who you want to be. That is all you can bring. Yes, you might be filled with the joy of the moment; yes, you may have this mental picture of what the marriage is going to be; yes, you may have expectations of what your life is going to be like after you are married. The reality is *you bring to the marriage who you are.*

Marriage doesn't guarantee happiness. It involves two people, who love themselves, coming together to share who they are with the other. If there is no self-love, there will be unrealistic expectations. If there is no self love, there will be an expectation of being taken care of. If you don't have good feelings about you, you will bring your unhealthy self-emotions into the marriage. It won't take long for that to wear on the emotion of love.

Marriage doesn't guarantee happiness. It simply provides you with the opportunity to blend personalities and offer your partner the best of you. As long as each are offering their best, there is the strengthening of love. Understand giving your best today will make the relationship even better tomorrow. As long as each is personally growing, they are focusing the relationship on improvement. With improvement in the relationship comes joy; with joy comes happiness; with happiness comes a continual searching on how to make the relationship even better. As long as that is the process, the relationship has a solid foundation to continue to build upon.

Here are some questions for you to answer *honestly*:

- *Are you happy with the way your relationship is right now?*

- *What is the #1 thing you could improve that would make the relationship even better?*

- *Are you happy with you?*

How Do You Grow The Happiness?
G *get real about what is happening*
R *refuse to avoid issues*
O *open yourself to taking risks*
W *work with each other*

BLANK CHECK
Love is an emotion you express,
not something you buy.

I stood in the automobile showroom and watched as she leaned over, kissed her dad on the cheek and said, "Dad, if you really love me, you will buy this car for me."

He looked at her, smiled and told the salesperson, "We'll take the car."

What a concept! "If you love me, you will buy me this car." What kind of a message does that send? One of the great tragedies of our time is the deterioration of the true meaning of love. What does it say when to prove you love someone you have to give them things? How does that prepare a child to understand the meaning of love? They grow up thinking that love is demonstrated by someone giving them things in the name of love. They don't seem to have a healthy definition of love as an emotion.

Paul came to see me while I was on the staff of First Baptist Church. He was a highly successful stockbroker in Palm Beach. His day began before the sun came up and didn't end until well after the sun went down. He and Price had been married for ten years and had one son, Scott, who was fourteen. I could tell by the way Paul entered my office he needed to talk, but he was also in a hurry. From what I knew about him that was the way he lived his life.

"Richard, I've only got a few minutes and I need to talk to you about Scott. I am not sure what I am going to do about his behavior. He is out of control and his mother and I are worried about him."

Let me tell you a little about Scott. At the age of

91

Once you start buying love, you have to continue and the price keeps going up.

eleven, Scott started receiving a weekly allowance of $500. Yes, the numbers are correct — $500 a week. Can you imagine an eleven year old with $500 every Monday in his pocket? There were no conditions to what he did with it; it was his to spend. The interesting thing was by Thursday morning Scott was broke. There were no drugs, no booze. Scott spent his money buying his friends. He would buy lunch for them, pay for them to play games and spend it in order to make sure he had friends around his life.

Now, back to my conversation with his father. "Paul," I said. "I don't think the issue is really Scott."

Those words made him sit up in his chair. "I don't understand what you are saying. He has become a handful, and we are at our wits end. His mother is really stressed out over the entire situation. We need your help!"

"Paul, I agree you need my help, but not with Scott. You need my help with what the two of you are doing to this child."

I could tell by the redness of his neck this was not the conversation he came to me to have. I knew there was part of him that wanted to get up and storm out of my office, but the other part wanted to know what I was talking about.

"I don't understand what you are saying. Are you suggesting that Price and I are bad parents? Is that what you are talking about?"

"No, you are not bad parents, but you are misguided parents. Paul, look at what you are teaching Scott. He is eleven and has a weekly allowance of $500 with no restrictions on what he does with it. How many eleven-year-old children do you know who get that type of allowance? Why are you doing that?"

93

The look on his face stated even stronger he was not happy with this conversation. He stared at me for a few minutes and then continued.

"When I was growing up, we didn't have anything. I wore my older brothers clothes he had outgrown. I went to school and the kids made fun of me. We were poor and I vowed I wouldn't live that way, nor would my family. I don't want Scott to go through what I went through growing up."

"That's a noble thought, but it is dangerous to the development of your son. Paul, you are a good provider, but you are creating a child who will be emotionally crippled by your behavior."

The look on his face said he didn't understand what I was saying. I paused long enough to allow him to emotionally catch up and then continued.

"Love is an emotion you share, not something you buy. What you and Price are doing is buying your son. The only thing he understands is you pay him to be your child. What do you think that is going to do to him as an adult? Do you think he will understand how to love someone? Do you think he will be able to really feel love and know what he is feeling? What about his understanding of money? Do you think he will understand money and a work ethic?"

I could tell by the look on his face he was beginning to understand what I was talking about. The redness that had taken over his neck went away and he moved forward emotionally into the conversation.

"We have never meant to hurt Scott."

"I know that. You are using your yesterday to protect him. That is good and bad. It is good that you want him to have a great life. It is bad when you are using unhealthy

94

techniques to teach him about living. You are going to have a real challenge on your hands. You have spoiled him and created a series of expectations that are going to be challenging to take away. He is accustomed to the money and being able to do what he wants with it. You are going to have to reverse what you have been doing and guide him to understanding that love is an emotion, not something you buy. Paul, you and Price have been buying your son, not really teaching him about love."

I spent a lot of time with Paul and Price working through how they were going to redesign their presence in their son's life. It took several years and a lot of heart to heart conversations with Scott, but together they worked through it.

Today Scott is 26 and living in Dallas. Recently, I received a letter from him. Here is part of what he said to me.

"For a long time I hated you. I knew you were the reason my life was being torn apart. I blamed you for the friends I lost. When mom and dad took my allowance away, the people I hung out with went away. I really hated you! But, now I would like to say a big *thank you* for what you did. I don't know where I would be today if we had continued on the track we were on. I know my life wouldn't be as good as it is today. Paula and I are very happy and very deeply in love with each other. I understand what you told dad that he kept repeating to me. Love is an emotion, not something you can buy. Thank you for being there and being honest with my parents. Thank you for helping me get a healthy view of love. I don't hate you any more."

I wish more parents would slow down and look at what they are doing to their children. They are teaching their children a definition of love through their behavior. When they overdo the presents at Christmas or on birthdays, they are sending a very negative message about love. Children need to feel the emotion, not see it through presents. Children need to be hugged and told, "I love you," not handed another toy or gift.

Adults need to understand the need to express love through words and emotions, not simply through gifts. I am not saying *don't give gifts*. Just examine the reason you are giving the gift.

One of my closest friends shared with me a situation that happened with his wife. Tom had always been one to spoil his wife. He enjoyed giving her the biggest and most expensive gifts. Recently, his business went through a financial time of restructuring. It meant his cash flow wasn't real strong and he knew it would mean readjusting his spending habits. Three months before his wife's birthday he started making a list of things she had said she would like to have. He was so excited to give them to her.

Her birthday arrived and when Sharon came down stairs all the presents were on the kitchen table. One by one, she opened them and when she finished he said he could see the disappointment on her face.

"What are these?" Were her words as she stared at each of them.

"These are the things you have said you would like to have. I made a list and have been getting them for you over the past few months."

"These are not birthday presents. What am I going to tell my friends when they ask what I got for my birthday? How will I tell them I got DVDs, videos, cds and a gift certificate? They are going to want to see the jewelry you got me. These are not birthday presents."

He didn't have to tell me how disappointed he was in her reaction. The pain in his eyes said it all.

"Richard," he said in a strained voice. "I have really spoiled her. To her it is not what I give her. It is how big and expensive it is. I was proud of the things I got her. It was all she had said she wanted."

"What did you do?"

"I told her those were my presents to her and I was sorry she didn't like them. I then picked them all up and returned them. If she didn't like what I had gotten her out of love, there were no presents."

He paused, looked at the floor and then said. "Once you start buying love, you have to continue and the price just keeps going up."

She didn't get it! Love is an emotion you share, not something you buy. When love becomes something that is defined by gifts, it loses its strength and makes people question the strength of the relationship. When love becomes a blank check, you will never have enough to fill in the blank. Love is an emotion, not a stack of gifts. Many don't know how to share the emotion, so they give gifts. I wish they could see the danger to what they are doing. My friend was right! *Once you start buying love, you have to continue and the price just keeps going up.* In the long run that will destroy the real meaning of love. In the long run it devalues the emotions and weakens presence.

Here are some questions for you to answer *honestly*:

- *Do you measure love by the gifts you are given?*
- *What do you do to express your love?*
- *If you got nothing but "I love you" for your birthday, would that be enough?*

What Really Says "I Love You?"

L *lots of mental, emotional and physical hugs*
O *openly supporting one another's dream*
V *very strong communication*
E *emotional presence*

You Can Run, But You Can't Hide
Avoidance doesn't resolve anything.

Here is a truth most don't understand. *Everything you think you are running from, you are actually running toward.* I have always been amazed how most believe you can avoid an issue and it will just go away. Whoever started that fairy tale didn't live in the real world. Avoidance doesn't do away with issues. Oh, they may hide in a dark corner, *but* they are simply waiting to hit you with a surprise attack. Avoidance doesn't resolve anything.

Have you and your spouse ever started a conversation of disagreement about one issue and before you were finished had five or six other issues laying on the table? Then, what do you do? You look at each other and ask, "How did we get here?"

Avoidance doesn't resolve anything. Avoidance guarantees you will have to face the issue again. All avoidance does is store the issue in your inner emotional vault of unresolved issues. All have this vault; all store incomplete emotional issues inside; all have the vault come open and the unresolved issue emotionally take over their behavior. When that happens, you are not about resolving anything; you are about punishing the other person.

Why do so many people choose to avoid, rather than confront issues they know can emotionally tear things apart?

Many do it because they don't like confrontation. Do you like confrontation? When something needs to be confronted, will you step up and face it? If you don't, what do you think happens to it? It gets placed in your inner emotional vault of unresolved issues.

99

Conflict is the result of unresolved issues.

It is important you understand confrontation is one of the most important communication tools you need to master. It is not about losing or winning a disagreement. Confrontation is about finding a common agenda that allows you to resolve the issue. It is the common agenda that keeps you focused on resolving the issue. If each has their own agenda and is unwilling to listen to the other, there is just more confusion, which adds to the frustration that ends up with two people at war.

Many have told me *they just don't like conflict.* It is easier for them to walk away than stay and address the issue. What they fail to understand is conflict is the result of unresolved issues. Conflict feeds the disappointment, which adds to the frustration that just makes a person more angry. Conflict only goes away when issues have been resolved. Without the resolution, conflict grows into discontentment. That just adds fuel to the fire that is burning because of all the unresolved issues stored in the vault.

Ken and Debbie are a perfect example. Ken grew up with a mother who talked about confronting issues, but really attacked the people who didn't agree with her. He learned at an early age *it is safer to just keep your mouth shut.* In one of our sessions he said, "My mother and I were having this disagreement. It was all about something she had done that was wrong. She knew she was wrong; I knew she was wrong, but there was no way she was going to admit she was wrong. When I point blank questioned her statement, she slapped me and told me not to ever question her again. That was all it took. From then on I just kept my mouth shut. Her idea of confronting issues was you sitting there while she told you how wrong you were and how right she was. There was no discussion. There

101

was only her way."

"How did your dad handle your mom?" Was my next question for him.

"My dad hid from my mom. He didn't question what she said or did. He just played silent and dumb. That is how he survived in the relationship."

Debbie was the type that let her temper out every time she got upset. You knew what was going on inside her. She didn't let it out in a calm fashion. She would scream, fuss and cry.

Put Ken and Debbie together and what type of communication do you think they had? It was nonexistent. Something would happen, Debbie would scream and Ken would withdraw and hide inside himself. That would drive Debbie up the wall. So, she would just get louder and louder. Put that behavior as the common routine of dealing with issues and what do you think happened after ten years of marriage. Both of their inner emotional vaults were full and running over. There was no more room for any new issues.

Ken decided he had had all he could take of her. "I cannot take her tactics any more. She has killed any feelings I have had for her. I hate going home; I hate being around her. She has become a very ugly person to me. I just want out of the hell. I want a divorce."

Debbie had had all she could take of Ken. "I cannot stand his silence. There are times I want to kill him. He won't talk; he just sits there and stares at me. I have had all of this I can take. I want out. I want a divorce."

In our sessions I worked to show Debbie how her behavior reminded Ken of his mother. Well, she didn't want to be compared to that woman.

102

"I am not like her," was her common statement. "She is a witch and I am not like that. All I have ever wanted was for him to talk to me. If I was important to his life, he would talk to me."

I worked to show Ken that Debbie's behavior triggered his old tapes about his mother. Each time Debbie would attack, he would emotionally race back to his childhood and relive his mother's behavior.

"You are right!" Were his words. "When she starts the screaming, all I can see is my mother standing in front of me. I just want to run away. I want to get far away from her."

To compound the issue Ken had found a young lady who didn't scream. She was quiet and didn't push him to talk. He looked at Debbie and then looked at this other woman and she looked a lot more attractive. Each time Debbie would get upset, he would run to the other woman.

When I confronted him about the affair, he justified it with "but she understands me. She doesn't push and scream. She just lets me be me."

"Ken," I asked. "Do you realize you are running to her to avoid being around Debbie? Do you see what you are doing? When you and Debbie got married, you saw it as an opportunity to get away from your mother. What you don't realize is because you didn't resolve the issues you had with your mother, you simply found another personality just like her. Debbie is the same behavioral type as your mother."

The look on his face told me this was not what he wanted to hear. "She wasn't like that in the beginning. She was calm and we had fun together."

"Yes! But you were dating. You were both on your best behavior. You rushed into getting married so you could get away from your mother. You only dated for six months before you ran off and got married. You didn't know her and she didn't know you."

I paused to let all this soak in. "Ken, tell me what you see when you look at her parents?"

"Her mother rules the house. Her father is very silent and either goes along or just disappears."

"Does that remind you of another relationship you know?"

"Yes! My parents' relationship. I see what you are saying. I married my mother."

I put the same question to Debbie. "Deb, when you look at Ken's parents, what do you see?"

"I see a crazy woman and a very scared man. They don't talk. She screams and he hides. I don't know how they have made it this long."

"Debbie, does that in any way remind you of your parent's relationship?"

There was a long pause. "Yes it does. It reminds me of my parents. My mother was the vocal one, and my dad just avoided dealing with or listening to her. I wonder how they have made it this far."

"Debbie, do you see any of your mother's behavior in you?"

Man, did that strike a cord. She turned white and then red. The look on her face told me this was not something she wanted to talk about.

"Debbie," I said. "This is important. Do you see any of your mother's behavior in you?"

"This is hard to talk about. The one thing I have always said is I don't want to be like my mother. Yet, when I look at me, I have become just like her. Ken has become like my father and his father. This is not a pretty picture."

"Do you understand for ten plus years the two of you have been avoiding facing the obvious? Your marriage has become the repeat of those of your parents. They gave you the example; you swore you wouldn't repeat that, but guess what you have done?"

It took a lot of work on both of their parts, but we were able to put their relationship together with a different design. Ten years of avoiding doesn't get resolved over night. It wasn't easy for them, but when they realized what they had done and were doing, it caused them to slow down and face their behavior.

Ken broke his silence and Debbie learned how to be calmer in her presentation of herself. Their marriage isn't perfect, but they are growing and learning to be with each other, rather than looking at each other and seeing their parents.

Avoidance doesn't resolve anything. All it does is feed the disharmony and push people further apart. The further apart you become the easier it is to justify your behavior by pointing a finger at the other person's actions. That is simply another form of avoidance.

Here are some questions for you to answer *honestly*:

- *How good are you at confronting issues?*

- *Are there any issues you are avoiding right now?*

- *Is avoiding issues causing any conflict in your relationship?*

105

How Do You Learn To Overcome Your Fear of Confrontation?

L *listen with your ears and eyes, not emotions*
E *emotionally know the need*
A *always take responsibility for your actions*
R *refuse to use silence as an answer*
N *never give yourself permission to run away*

WHO AM I?

*It's not about changing each other; it is about learning
to blend personalities.*

You really do have to believe God has a sense of humor.
Look around and see all the things that happen. The greatest
demonstration is marriage. He put man and woman together
on this earth to live harmoniously. Now, how often does that
happen?

Don't you find the entire concept of marriage
interesting? Two people meet; there is this attraction; they fall
in love; one asks the other to marry them, and they say, "I do."
Then, the real fun starts.

Too many times dating is a game. Too many are
searching for "that one and only special person" for their life.
Well, let me tell you what I believe. There is not just one!
There are three. That's right. There are seven who will enter
your life you could marry that could make you happy for a
while. There are three that will enter your life you could marry
that would complete your life. Sound strange?

The reason so many struggle with marriage is *they
married one of the seven and didn't wait for one of the three to
enter their life.* That means they have settled. The result will be
the lack of fulfillment in the relationship. When you settle, you
get a person. When you find one of the three, you get a partner.

Casey had just walked away from a relationship that
was headed for the marriage altar. The question had been
asked, the "yes" had been given, and everything was in place
for the big day. *Yet,* there was something wrong and both
of them knew it, but neither wanted to admit it. Finally, she
listened to her heart and not her emotions and did what she

Relationships at their easiest are challenging.

knew she had to do. She broke it off!

I met Casey at a seminar I was doing in St. Louis. She was standing at my product tools table reading one of my poetry books with tears streaming down her face. You couldn't miss her. She was this strikingly beautiful young lady with one of my books in her hand just sobbing. I walked over, paused for a moment and asked her, "Are you okay?"

She looked up and the look said, "Dummy, can't you see I am not okay." She brushed some tears away and in a soft uncontrolled whisper said, "This hits too close to home. I just ended a relationship that had been off and on for years. We were going to be married in a few weeks, but I couldn't go through with it."

Watching her eyes refill with tears, I took her arm and led her to a couple of chairs where we could talk without the whole group watching her cry.

"Thanks," she said. "I feel like such an idiot. There are days I just cannot stop crying."

"Don't call yourself an idiot for letting your feelings out. That takes strength."

"I really do love him, but I know I couldn't marry him and be happy. We were so different. We wanted different things. When we first got together, I thought he was God's answer for my life. Everyone told me we were perfect for each other. This was going to be a marriage made in heaven. I wanted that to be true, so I stopped being me in order to become what he wanted me to be. That was when I began to question what I was doing. The more I gave up being me the less attention I got from him. It was as if I was a pretty trophy to hang on his arm. It seemed he had won and now there was no need to pay attention to me anymore."

There was this long pause while she gathered herself emotionally. She didn't have to say it; you could feel the pain that was shooting through her.

"Richard, I knew I didn't want to live my life that way. I knew this was going to be the way he wanted it to be, and I wasn't going to settle. I have seen too many of my friends get married and struggle with the fact they had given up their life. I won't do that!"

"Did the two of you talk about what you were feeling?"

"Let's see, *talk*? To him there was nothing to talk about. He had what he wanted. It didn't matter if I was happy or not. He had his relationship."

"Did he understand when you broke off the engagement?"

"No! He couldn't figure out what had happened to me. He thought I had lost it. He went to my parents and asked them what was wrong. I tried to share with him what I was going through and it didn't make any sense to him. All that did was show me that my decision had been correct."

The thing that impressed me the most about Casey was the fact she was not willing to settle for a relationship. She wanted a relationship where she was a partner, not a relationship where she was a trophy and a prisoner.

I'll say it again. *Relationships at their easiest are challenging.* It is not as simple as saying "I do." A relationship is two individuals coming together as partners. I don't believe in the strict concept of "oneness" that many teach. If two people are to become one, one has to become less in order for the other to become more. That is not partnership; that is a form of slavery. The important issue here must be togetherness. It must be two people together in purpose, in spirit and in commitment. This is the only way there will be the common agenda that allows them to move forward through the changing terrain of the relationship.

This means it is not about two people coming together and one expecting the other to change to meet their requirements. It is about two individuals learning to take their uniqueness of personality and blend them together into a design that allows them to accept each other as an individual.

Too many enter their marriage expecting to change or expecting the other person to change to become more of what they *need* them to be. All that does is weaken the foundation of the relationship and make two people strangers, rather than allowing them to move closer together.

When I was on the staff of First Baptist Church in West Palm, I did several of the weddings. Now, if I was doing your wedding, you had to have four sessions with me:

- Session #1: The Couple
- Session #2: The Groom
- Session #3: The Bride
- Session #4: The Couple

My favorite session was with the Bride. I would have the groom bring her. We would chat for a few minutes, and then I would ask him to leave us alone for an hour. I always took joy in watching the look on the groom's face when I told him to leave us alone. You would have thought I had created pain for him.

"It's okay," I would say. "We will just be an hour. Come back then."

After he had left I would tell the young bride, "I need your help." I would hand her this sheet of paper that had five blanks on it. The top would read <u>Things I Plan On Changing In</u>

111

Him After We Are Married.

There would be this look of surprise on her face, but she would fill out the list. The average young lady would list seven. One night I had this lady list thirty-one and ask for more paper.

What I was looking for were points of confusion that were going to create emotional collisions before they had had the time to adjust to each other. It didn't matter whether the couple had lived together or not, there were always going to be emotional collisions over behavior. Most were the result of expectations that hadn't been discussed. Many young brides have this idea they can make their man into the man they want them to be. That creates emotional collisions that build walls between the couple. Many young grooms expect their bride to take care of them like their mother did. That creates emotional walls that result in emotional collisions.

They both need to understand *it is not about changing each other; it is about blending personalities.* Yes, people can improve, but you are not going to change them. It has to be their doing, not someone else forcing them.

Here are some questions for you to answer *honestly*:

- *Are there things you would like to change in your mate?*
- *Do you ever feel your spouse is trying to change you?*
- *Do you and your spouse have very different personalities?*

112

How Do You Learn To Blend Personalities?

B *believe in your spouse*
L *love the person they are*
E *environment is growth for both*
N *notice their strengths and good qualities*
D *don't work to reinvent them*

Put The Gloves On
Couples that don't fight don't grow.

I grew up watching three very interesting families on
TV — "Ozzie & Harriett Nelson," "Leave It To Beaver" and
"Father Knows Best." I think the thing I remember the most
about these three shows is none of them ever fought. Mom and
dad never fought! They never raised their voice to each other;
they never had a good old knock down drag out fight that most
couples have.

They were not like the "Honeymooners" or the
Bunkers. These four were always at each other's throats. The
TV sitcom, *All In The Family*, really changed the face of TV.
Archie tackled issues that had always been taboo for TV. The
thing that made the show so popular was the fact it was real
life.

Archie and Edith had a very unique relationship.
Mix their relationship with Mike and Gloria and you had the
makings of one mixed up family. They could even be classified
as dysfunctional.

Archie and Edith were always going at it; Archie and
Mike were always in a shouting match; Gloria and Mike had
their share of fights. Edith and Gloria seemed to be the only
two that had a civil relationship with each other. Get the men
out of the picture and there was peace and tranquility.

TV audiences loved the radical closed-minded views of
Archie. They may not have agreed with him, but they tuned in
show after show to hear him share his philosophies about life.
Many felt sorry for Edith and applauded her when she stood
her ground with the male chauvinist Archie Bunker. They were
the real deal.

115

If you don't fight, you will end up at war with each other. Someone will get killed!

I don't know why the television industry was afraid of real life. I don't know why they felt they had to paint this picture of the perfect marriage. Everyone knows in real life marriage is not perfect. To have a perfect marriage you have to have perfect people, and I haven't met that couple yet. In real life couples have disagreements; in real life they fight!

I am one who believes that fighting is healthy. Couples that don't fight don't grow. For a couple to have no disagreements means they don't discuss issues.

I remember one night meeting this couple. I had just finished doing my program, <u>If Marriages Are Made In Heaven, Why Can't They Be Endured On Earth?</u> Their opening words to me were very interesting. "Know what? We had a very difficult time identifying with what you were talking about tonight."

They paused to see what kind of a reaction they would get from me. "Really," was my response back to them. "What made the material challenging to identify with?"

"Oh, we don't fight."

"How long have the two of you been married?"

"We've been married for seven years."

"And in that seven years you have never had a fight?"

"No, we haven't."

Here is what was interesting about that conversation. He did all the talking. She never said a word. The look on her face was one of total embarrassment. I thought to myself, "If they haven't had a fight up to now, I think they will when they get home."

I looked at the two of them and said, "Can I ask you a couple of questions?"

"Sure. What would you like to ask us?"

117

"If you don't fight, what do you do when you disagree with each other?"

"Oh, if that happens, we just don't talk anymore about it."

"That solves the issue?"

"It just doesn't come up again. We made a pact when we got married that if we couldn't agree on an issue, we would just not deal with it."

The look on my face must have told them I was having a challenge with what he was saying. I looked at her, then at him and said, "Not talking about issues works. You just pretend they don't exist, and there is no emotional aftermath to that?"

Finally, she couldn't take it anymore. "He is not telling you the whole story. If the issue is about him, we don't talk about it. It is closed and not to be brought up again. If the issue is about me or one of the kids, he brings it up. There is no discussion; we just listen to what he has to say. We don't fight because we are not allowed to talk."

I wish you could have seen the look on his face. He was hot! For some reason they had to go. They didn't have time to discuss this anymore. I would have loved to have been a fly on the wall in their house that night. I bet she let him have it. Everything that she had held back probably came out with forceful energy.

Couples need to fight. They need to get their disagreements out and face the emotional upheaval they are facing.

What couples don't need to do is have war. They don't need to get in a destructive situation where their mission is to destroy the other person. That is not fighting; that is war.

You cannot live with someone without having

emotional collisions. You cannot live with another person without having times when you are upset and frustrated with each other. Those times are going to happen. When they do happen, you either bury them or you address them. If you could stay emotionally calm and address everything with your mind leading the way, then yes — you might not fight. But, you are human and humans have emotions. You are human and humans are going to have emotional collisions. That is not bad; it is just a fact of marriage. You need to put the gloves on and fight. I don't mean you physically punch each other. What you do is verbally spar with each other.

It is important you understand the difference between having a fight and going to war. Fights are the result of temper; war is the result of anger. Fights are about expressing your feelings and being heard; wars are about attacking and not wanting to listen. Fighting doesn't create casualties; wars are about creating casualties.

Let me share with you some guidelines for having a healthy fight:

#1: Don't use the words "you always" or "you never." No one always or never does anything.

#2: Don't use yesterday as the reason for the fight. Yesterday opens too many old closets.

#3: Don't fight inside the house. You will fight dirtier inside the house. Go out for a walk through your neighborhood. You will be amazed how calmly you will walk past your neighbor's house. Go out for dinner. Once you are seated, go from table to table, give them a ballot, tell them you are going to have a fight and ask them to vote on who wins.

#4: When you are wrong, admit it; when you are right, shut up. How many times have you seen one gloat in the fact they were right and the other one was wrong. It is not about being right or wrong; it is about resolving the situation.

#5: <u>Don't put others in the middle</u>. When you do, you are asking someone to tell you you are right. Don't do that to your friends. It is involving people in your personal affairs who shouldn't be there.

#6: <u>Don't use humor as a way of getting even</u>. One night I was at a party in Palm Beach and there was this couple present whose demeanor said they were not happy. He had had a little too much to drink and decided to use the party to say some things to his wife. He was on a roll; he was poking fun at her and had everyone, except her, in stitches. I happened to see him the next day and his left arm was in a cast. He told me he had fallen; I think she went home and beat the stuffing out of him. Most who use humor to say things in jest are actually saying what they really feel.

#7: <u>Don't avoid conflict with the silent treatment</u>. Have you ever asked your spouse if something was wrong and got a cold "NO!" You knew differently. Their behavior said there was something not right. Have you ever been told "we'll talk about it later" and knew it was a closed subject? What about being told "it's nothing" when you knew it was a big deal.

Silence doesn't solve anything. It just files issues away in the inner vault of unresolved conflict. That vault will come open. When it does, you will not be able to control the rush of emotions that come out. At this point it will not be about fighting; it will be about going to war. You will not care about resolving things; you will only want to make sure you cause pain.

Over the years, I have watched the vault come open in counseling situations. Issues that have been filed away have turned to rage. Their appearance is a full out assault designed to seek and destroy. Every person in a relationship knows one thing they can say to their mate that will totally destroy them. They use their ugly weapon when they want to sink the other one emotionally. It is not a shot fired to hurt, but one fired to destroy.

The reality is *if you don't fight, you will have war.* Most relationships that wear down and out are the result of couples who didn't fight. They just stored all their emotional pain until the inner vault was full. Then, it sprang open and the war was on. In all wars, someone is going to get mortally wounded. Those emotional wounds don't heal. Learn how to fight, and then enjoy making a peace treaty. The negotiations could be a lot of fun.

Here are some questions for you to answer *honestly*:

- *Do you fight or have war?*
- *Are you good at communicating disappointments?*
- *How full is your inner vault of unresolved issues?*

How Do You Learn To Fight, Not Have War?
 F *face issues head on; don't avoid them*
 I *inwardly don't seek to win; resolve*
 G *get clear on the need for the discussion*
 H *hold hands while you talk*
 T *take it one issue at a time*

121

WHO'S AT FAULT?
Issues don't create conflict; agendas do.

When you think about the challenges of a
relationship, most will talk about their struggle with the lack
of communication as one of the major issues. When you
read books on relationships, they talk about the need for
communication. Everywhere you turn people want to make
communication the beginning and the ending for dealing with
the challenges that couples face.

I agree that communication is important, but in
my mind it is not the major issue. Yes, there is a need for
communication; yes, there is a need for couples to share,
but simply talking or sharing does not mean they are
communicating.

I have seen so many couples that spend hours talking
only to walk away with more confusion than they started
with. The result is the lack of resolution which means the
conversation will have to happen all over again.

When you are continually dealing with the same issues
over and over, there are several different negative emotions that
get involved. There is the feeling the other person doesn't care.

I have heard this statement over and over. "They must
not care or they would listen. I get so frustrated having to
repeat myself over and over." The real issue here may not be
that they are not listening.

I have heard this statement on numerous occasions.
"If they really loved me, we wouldn't still be dealing with
this issue. They know how important this is to me. I must not
matter very much." Again, the real issue may not have anything
to do with them not caring.

123

*All lives collide
at the point of
agendas!*

There is also this statement that keeps being vocalized. "I am so frustrated with them. I cannot get them to understand how I feel. I have talked until I am blue in the face and it is still there unresolved. I cannot talk about this anymore." Anything that is talked about, but not resolved is going to result in frustration and a sense of doubt.

There is also the negative feelings of not being valued in the relationship. This is the common statement I have heard over the years. "I must not matter very much. He/she doesn't pay attention to anything I say. It is like I am talking to a brick wall."

When you feel devalued in the relationship, your entire view of the relationship takes on a negative sight plan. That results in even more negative feelings that cause you to withdraw even more. That means more reactions and less resolution.

It also attracts worry and doubt. These are much more dangerous than the others. These two emotions are foundation eaters. Once they enter the relationship, they begin to erode the foundation of trust. As trust begins to diminish, the doubts and the worry blossom and begin to grow and take root in other aspects of the relationship.

Yes, communication is important, *but* the lack of communication is a symptom of a much bigger issue. That issue is the lack of agenda management. Communication demands that all participants be searching for a resolution, rather than a win. It means that all involved must want to get beyond this stumbling block, rather than walking away feeling they have won.

The challenge here is setting your emotions aside and allowing your mind to find the resolution that allows everyone to walk away feeling good about what has happened. That will not happen without a common agenda. That will not happen without everyone being on the same mental page.

The opposite of resolution is confusion. How damaging is confusion to a relationship? What happens if the issues that need to be resolved are just being fed a continual diet of confusion? What does that do to the relationship? Does it wear the people out? Does it heighten the feeling of disappointment? Do disappointments just go away or do they attach themselves to other emotions and create a chain of reactionary events? You have been there and you know the answers to these questions. The message here is simple, but often missed. *Issues don't create conflict; agendas do.* If you can grasp this and apply it to your life, you will find an interesting result. Things get resolved and life moves forward, rather than in circles.

All human lives collide at the point of agendas, not issues. To simply stare at the issue and not focus on the agenda each is bringing with them is to guarantee there will be confusion, frustration and the lack of resolution. That means the conversation goes on and in doing so attracts and attaches more negative emotions. The result is a life lost in the circle of sameness.

No greater illustration has ever been handed my life than that of Miram and David. They got married not understanding what marriage was. Each was running away from an unhealthy home life, which was attached to their need for emotional attention. They thought that meant they loved each other and got married. That was twenty-two years prior.

They both admitted they knew within the first year this was a dangerous relationship, but neither were willing to share their true feelings. So, over the years they stored their feelings in their inner vault of unresolved issues. Year after year, they continued to add to the vault. Each time it would come open they would go to war with the desire to hurt each other.

Each time they tried to talk, David would arrive with his agenda and Miram with hers. They constantly interrupted each other. Most of the time one didn't get to finish what they were saying, because the other would barge in with their anger stated as disagreement.

Each had threatened to leave and file for divorce, but there were two children involved. There was also the fact each had come from divorced parents and neither wanted to go through that.

My first assessment of the two of them was *they really did love each other, but had never had a good example of a healthy relationship.*

In my meeting with David he told me, "I love her. I just cannot live with her anymore. She has become impossible and unreasonable."

In my meeting with Miram she told me, "I love him, but I cannot live with him anymore. He has become an ugly person who tries to hurt me in every way possible. I am tired of the emotional torture he puts me through."

I had each prepare a list of their hurts, frustrations and pains they felt in the relationship. I had them give their list to me without discussing them with each other. I took the lists, found the common items on each list and brought them back together.

In our time together, I told them these were the rules for our time together:

    #1:   *They had to allow me to lead the discussion.*
    #2:   *They could not change the subject until*

	I said it was okay.
#3:	*They could not interrupt the other person while they were talking.*
#4:	*Neither would be allowed to dominate the conversation. Their responses were limited to no more than seven minutes.*
#5:	*Personal attacks or blame were not allowed.*

They both reluctantly agreed to the rules.

At our first meeting, I handed each of them the agenda for the meeting. It was a sheet of paper with one statement on it. They looked at it, looked at each other and David asked, "What is this?"

"That's our agenda for this meeting."

"But, there is only one thing listed here. We have a lot more issues than this."

"I know, but this is our agenda for this meeting."

Miram looked at David, looked at me and said. "I don't understand. I thought you were going to help us work through our issues."

"I am and this is our agenda for this meeting."

They looked at each other and said, "Okay."

For the first hour of our time I had to keep reminding them of the rules they had agreed to. Their tendency was to slip back to their old behavior. They would interrupt; they would use one statement to lash out about another issue; they would emotionally attack the other; on a couple of occasions each threatened to leave. If it had not been so serious, it would have been very humorous.

It took eighteen months to get through their issues. Each time they would arrive, I would hand them a sheet of paper with one issue on it. We would spend our time working through that one issue.

About five months into our time together they arrived in my office laughing. I asked them, "What is so funny?"

They looked at each other and just cracked up with laughter. "Richard," David said, "You are beginning to rub off on us. At home if we start talking, we take a sheet of paper and write the issue we are going to talk about. We follow the same rules there as we do here. Oh, we know you are not present, but we pretend you are sitting in the chair across from us and we swear we can hear your voice directing us. This idea of creating an agenda and following it really works."

David was correct. "This idea of an agenda really works." Issues bring us together; it is the establishing of a common agenda that allows you to resolve it. If there is no common agenda, there will be individual agendas. The individual agenda guarantees confusion. Confusion guarantees the weakening of the relationship. The common agenda is what allows you to resolve, solve and move forward.

Here are some questions for you to answer *honestly*:

- *Do you ever not listen because you are not on the same page of thought?*
- *Do you need to establish a common agenda?*
- *Are there points of confusion in your relationship that need to be resolved?*

129

How Do You Follow The Common Agenda?

A *agree upon the issue for discussion*
G *get clear on why this is an issue*
E *enter with your emotions in check*
N *never interrupt the other person*
D *direct points of confusion with questions*
A *always seek resolution, not victory*

UNTIL DEATH DO US PART
Divorce doesn't end a relationship;
it just changes the residences.

In the 50's, 60's and 70's when people got married, they believed this was a life commitment. They were not naive enough to believe it was going to be an easy journey. But, they were committed to the relationship and working through the rough times.

That all changed in the mid 80's when divorce became an acceptable exit. Rather than working through the tough times together, it became easier to give up, walk away and find another person to fill the emotional void the breakup had created.

I am not sure society fully understands the damage no fault divorce has created. No longer did people feel it was worth the energy to work it out; it was now okay to throw away what they once thought was a relationship they were willing to commit their life to.

Granted, I believe there are some couples where divorce is the best option. When there is no desire to work through or when the marriage is a piece of paper not a commitment or when one party has proven through behavior they don't love the other person, then they should not spend the rest of their life working to destroy the other person.

As much as we might not like to admit it, unhappy people work to make other people unhappy. People who don't want to be a part of something prove that fact with their behavior. People who don't love their spouse prove that through their actions. Over a period of time it wears on the relationship. Over a period, it wears on the positive spirit from

131

Time and distance heals,
but it doesn't erase memories.

all the people. Over a period of time it can make those who have been friends, strangers. When those who have been "in love" simply "love" each other, it changes the entire design of the relationship.

I met Mark at the conclusion of a program I was doing in central Pennsylvania. I was packing up when I noticed this man standing in the back of the room watching me. After 25+ years on the speaking tour, you learn to recognize when people want to talk to you, but don't have the courage to approach. I continued to pack and motioned him to join me. Knowing if I stopped packing it would scare him, I continued to pack as he approached. I motioned to him to sit, which he did.

"I guess you figured out I wanted to talk to you?"

"Yes," I said. "I have a few minutes if you want to talk."

"I do, but I don't know where to start. There is so much going on in my life I don't know where to start. I get up every day confused. I get up with good intentions, but get side tracked with all the things inside me that confuse me and keep me totally exhausted."

"What do you consider to be the number one issue you are dealing with?"

"It is my marriage. That has been my #1 issue for years."

I could tell by the emotions in his eyes he had been staring at this for years. He didn't have to tell me the pain he was going through. I could see it in his behavior. He looked away to keep me from seeing the tears that were running down his face. He stood up, walked away for a minute and then returned with his head down.

When he looked up, I knew it was okay to continue.

133

"Relationships can become very complicated. The thing that seems to complicate them the most are the unresolved issues. They happen, they are not talked about and grow into larger and larger emotional complications."

"I know what you mean. My marriage has been messed up from the second week. I didn't want to get married; I knew it was wrong, but there was so much pressure from everyone around me. I sat with my parents and told them I shouldn't be getting married. They told me I was just nervous. It would be okay. I told my sister, who had introduced me to my wife, and she told me to grow up that there was no one better for me than Meg. I thought how could they all be wrong? There had to be something wrong with me."

I could see the hurt in his eyes turning to anger. He was inching forward in his chair and his gestures were getting wider and wider.

"I wasn't wrong," were his next words. "I can honestly tell you I am not in love, nor have I ever been in love with her. I find myself looking at her and wondering why I ever married her."

"If that is true, why have you stayed married to her?"

"I have this thing about what I said in the marriage vows. I said I would stay until death do us part. I talked to my pastor about what that means and he told me it meant until one of us dies."

The puzzled look on his face told me he was still struggling with the concept of *until death do us part.* I knew he was looking to me for some words of wisdom.

I let him think for a minute and then I asked him, "Do you think you are alive in this relationship?"

The look on his face told me my question caught him

off guard. "What do you mean?"

"It's simple. Are you a whole person in the marriage? Does the marriage keep you charged with love and devotion?"

"Hell No! I am a piece of a person. I am not whole. In fact, I am more whole when I am on the road away from her. I am not in love with her. I don't want to be with or around her. Now, don't get me wrong. I haven't fooled around on her. I wouldn't do that, but I am not and haven't been attracted to her for years. In fact, we sleep in separate bedrooms. We first started because I snore so loud, but that decision sure took a lot of pressure off of me."

"So, back to my question. Do you think you are alive in this relationship?"

"No, I am a dead man who shows up and hangs out in the house when I have to be there."

"Do you think Meg is alive in this relationship?"

"No! In fact she has told me that most of the time she feels no life in our relationship."

"Now, stop and think about this question before you answer it. Do you feel you have worked to make this relationship work?"

There was a long pause. I could tell he was really thinking this through. "That's a good question. Several years ago we went through counseling at our church, but the person we talked to really didn't want to address any of our issues. They only wanted to tell us how we need to stay together no matter what. I listened and when I asked questions that were specific to our relationship, I didn't get any real answers. I only heard we had to stay together. How do you stay together with someone you are not really together with?"

"That's a good question. How do you?"

135

"I don't think you can. If you are not together, you are apart. Yes, we share the same house, but we live like strangers. Now that the kids are gone it is even worse. We don't even spend time in the same room together. I come home, go to my study, and stay there until I go to bed. She comes home and does her thing. We share a house; we don't live together."

"So, back to my original question. Do you think you are alive in this relationship? Would it be safe to say you are dead and the relationship is dead?"

"Yes!"

We have hurt so many people by teaching them they must stay in a relationship that is dead. I don't think God intended for anyone to stay dead while they are physically alive on the earth. I am not one who suggests divorce is the best option, but it must be something that is considered when there is no life in the relationship and no hope of breathing life back into it.

When people don't want the relationship, they are dead. When people are there, but not part of the relationship, the relationship is dead. To continue to kill each other is inhumane. Each would be better to remove the legal document of marriage and move forward with their life.

This should only be done after the couple has exhausted every possible means of working through their issues. The challenge is most don't deal with issues until they are a crisis. This allows time for the hurt and the pain to gain a suitcase filled with negative emotions.

These have laid in their vault of unresolved issues, festered and rotted. Anytime that vault comes open, it is not a pretty sight. All that comes out is directed in one direction — *to hurt the other person.* That will happen.

If divorce becomes the option, the couple needs to realize *divorce doesn't end the relationship; it just changes residences.* There will always be the emotional memories. You will never be totally free of what the experience meant to your life. Be that positive or negative, you will never be emotionally free from the experience.

It is amazing how you talk to people who have been divorced for years, and they will still mention their ex. You are never free from the emotional entanglements it created. Time and distance heal, but they don't erase memories. They are always present and capable of playing with your emotional makeup.

Here are some questions for you to answer *honestly*:

- *Are you totally in love with your spouse?*
- *Can you say your relationship is alive?*
- *Do you ever have memories about past relationships that play with your emotions?*

How Do You Keep a Relationship Alive?

A *address issues; don't let them fester*

L *look for positives; don't major on negatives*

I *invest time in continuing to date*

V *vary your routines; don't get in a rut*

E *emotional hugs a must*

ADULT CHILDREN
*Divorce punishes children when adults forget their
responsibility and act like children.*

Divorce will happen! As much as you may not like the
thought, divorce will happen. Lives are going to collide with
such an emotional impact; there will be no way to resolve it.
That means there will be a divorce.

The real tragedy is — *what it does to the other lives
that make up the relationship.* Children become the recipients
of so much of the emotional anger that the parents are feeling.
Too many times the children become the wedge to get even.

Recently, I was asked to sit with a couple who were
getting a divorce and talk to them about what their behavior
was doing to their two children. Denise was determined to
punish Walter. She knew how much he loved their two children
and knew she could get to him through denying him the right
to see the kids. They had joint custody, but that didn't mean
anything to her. When Walter would call to talk to the kids, she
would refuse to let him talk to them. Then, she would tell the
kids "Daddy didn't call." When Walter would get to see the
kids, they would ask, "Daddy, why didn't you call?" He would
tell them that he had called and didn't get to talk to them.

I asked Denise, "Why don't you let Walter talk to the
kids when he calls?"

She sat there, looked at him and then me. She didn't
say anything and I figured I had plenty of time to wait her out.
Finally she looked at me and said, "I am so angry at him. He
tore my whole life up. We had a good thing going and then, he
decided he didn't want me anymore. If he is going to tear my
life up, why shouldn't I do the same thing to him."

139

Children know what is happening, even if you pretend they don't.

"Denise, what about what this is doing to your two children?"

"They are young. They will live through it."

"Denise, isn't that cruel punishment for your kids? How can you do that to little lives who aren't old enough to understand what is going on?"

"Well, look at what he did to me! He didn't care about me. I just wanted us to stay together and have a family. He threw all that away."

What an angry woman! She didn't care what was happening to her children. All she wanted to do was use them to get even with him. Thank God that is not the rule, yet it happens more times than we know about.

Divorce will punish children when the adults forget their responsibility and act like children. If people just understood the emotional damage that does to these young lives. It creates permanent impressions they will struggle with the rest of their lives. In any divorce, the children are the lives that must be protected. Too many times they get caught in the emotional war that is going on between the adults that are acting like children.

The best illustration I have ever been handed happened while I was on the staff of First Baptist Church in West Palm Beach. Debbie and Randy decided after ten years of marriage it was over. They were separated when they started having a challenge with their nine-year-old son, Scott. He stopped talking. I mean totally stopped talking. They had tried everything; they took him to doctor after doctor and each time were told there was nothing physically wrong with him.

Finally, Debbie asked if I would try to help him. I told her to bring Scott and leave him with me for an hour. He arrived and Debbie wanted to stay. I told her "NO! I need to have time with him alone."

I knew Scott loved football, and I had this nerf football in my office. I said, "Scott, let's go out to the playground and throw the football around."

He got up and we walked to the church playground. "Scott, if you want to talk we can; if you don't, that's okay. We will just throw the ball. I will do whatever you want to do. I am here for you."

For the next forty-five minutes we threw the football. Scott didn't say a word. We went back to my office where his mother was waiting.

"Debbie, he didn't say anything. Would you bring him back to me tomorrow?"

"Yes, I will."

The next day Debbie and Scott arrived shortly after school. Debbie left and Scott and I walked to the playground where we spent the next thirty minutes throwing the football. The look in his eyes said he was in such deep pain.

"If you want to talk, I am willing to listen. If you don't, it's okay."

There were no words. I took him back to Debbie and asked her to bring him back the next day. The next day she arrived, left and Scott and I took our walk to the playground to throw the nerf football around.

I threw the ball to Scott. He caught it, squeezed it real tight to his chest and just burst out crying. He looked at me and said through his tears, "I didn't mean to; I didn't mean to."

"What Scott? What didn't you mean to do?"

"I didn't mean to chase my daddy off. I was bad and he left. I didn't mean to chase him off."

He came flying across the yard and leaped into my arms. He was sobbing as hard as I had ever seen any life cry. I hugged him and carried him back to my office. We sat until he stopped crying and I asked him, "Scott, would you like some ice cream?"

He nodded "yes" and I asked my secretary to take him to the church kitchen and get him some ice cream. After he had left my office, I got on the phone and called Debbie and Randy and told them to get to my office immediately.

They were there in a matter of a few minutes. They came racing in both asking, "Is Scott okay?"

"Yes, he is fine, but I don't think the two of you are anywhere close to being fine."

The look on their face told me they had no idea what I was talking about. I looked at each of them and asked, "What have you told Scott about what is happening between the two of you?"

They looked at each other and Randy was the one to answer. "We haven't told him much of anything. He is too young to understand. We thought it would be best to not drag him into the middle of our problem."

I shared with them what had happened and what Scott had said to me. Both of them sat there with tears in their eyes.

"We are so sorry. We didn't mean to hurt him. We just didn't want to create pain for him. We thought it would be better to work through this ourselves and then talk to him."

"You need to sit down with him and explain to him that he is not the problem. Randy, he is convinced you left because he was bad. Talk to him."

About that time Scott returned and Randy and Debbie

took him into the conference room and talked with him.

Divorce punishes children when the adults forget their responsibility and act like children. Too many times parents don't spend the time talking to the children about what has happened. They just walk away from the issue with them. That means the children must figure it out on their own. They don't have the emotional maturity to understand all that has taken place. If they are young, they tend to think it was something they had done. If they are older, they tend to look at their divorced parents and question whether they want to go through this thing called marriage.

Have you noticed how many young people are not dating? They do what they call cocooning. If they go out, they go out in groups. They don't pair off.

Children are humans who have emotions. Without experience and maturity, they don't understand what is happening. Therefore, they are left to figure it out on their own. In their groups they talk about their parents; they talk about what they think happened; they share emotions; they don't release them. When they finish sharing, they place them inside their emotional vaults.

If there are marital issues, don't pretend they are not happening. Children are smart enough to know when there are issues. Be open and honest with them. Involve them and don't try to protect them from what they are already questioning. If they ask questions, answer them. Don't blow them off. They are humans who have emotions.

Here are some questions for you to answer *honestly*:

- *Are you good at sharing with your children?*
- *Are you honest with your children?*
- *Are you adult about what happens in your life?*

How Does an Adult Act?
A *addresses issues they know are confusing*
D *doesn't play dumb about the truth*
U *understands their responsibility*
L *lives with love and concern*
T *they don't hurt those they love*

I Love You
"I love you" doesn't always mean
"I'm in love with you."

Language is an interesting study. There are so many words that are spoken that create a sense of confusion for those who are listening. Have you ever had someone talk to you and the terminology they were using wasn't being used the way you would use it? The result is you hearing one thing while they are saying something completely different. The result is a sense of confusion and in some cases disappointment with what has happened.

One of those words that gets lost in the translation is "Love." So much pain has been created because of the misuse of the word. So many misunderstandings have resulted from the misuse of the word.

I am not sure most know what they are saying when they say "I love you." I really don't believe most couples are in love with each other when they get married. Most don't fall in love until they have been married between three to five years.

If they are not in love, what do they have? They have this feeling of infatuation. They have found someone they feel comfortable with; they have found someone they think they can trust. Yet, they will not be certain until those dimensions are tested through spending married time with each other.

I have had many tell me, "We are going to live together to make sure we are compatible." Know what? Living together before you get married does not teach you whether you are compatible or not. It is just a way of playing house without the commitment to building the house. When there is no ceremony, there is no commitment. Without the ceremony, each is free to

147

Sex without the other aspects of love creates emotional confusion.

walk away. I know! The ceremony doesn't make you married, *but* it does create a sense of commitment.

I had a conversation with this young man about his commitment to the young lady he was living with. I asked him, "How long have you two been living together?"

"Four years."

"Have you thought about getting married?"

He chuckled, looked at me and said, "Why do I need to get married. I have the best of all worlds. I have someone to take care of me, someone to clean the house, sex when I want it and if it doesn't work, I can leave. Hey, without that piece of paper I am free to go anytime I want."

That's the challenge many face who choose to live together and not finalize the arrangement with marriage.

They may "love" each other, but not be "in love" with each other. The words "I love you" don't always mean, "I am in love with you."

This is where the Greeks help us so much. They understood better than us, the confusion the word "love" can create. So, rather than having one term for the word, they had three. They understood that some know how to use the word "love" to manipulate another; they understood that some are so starved to hear those three words; they will do anything to have someone tell them they love them.

The Greeks, also, understood that falling in love is a process, not something that just happens. They understood one could love, not be in love and not know the difference. They wanted the concept to be perfectly clear, so they gave us the three aspects of love to make you think about what you are saying.

The first of their three words is *Eros*. The term

149

translates to mean *physical attraction*. Most relationships get
their start because one person finds another person physically
attractive. Have you ever watched one person interview another
person with their eyes? They start at the top of the head and
work to the bottom of the feet with a few intermediate stops. If
they find the person physically attractive, they move forward.
It doesn't mean there is going to be a relationship, but all
relationships have to start at some point.

The tragedy of our society is with all the emphasis on
the physical. Too many get here and never get beyond this
point. Our society is sex crazy. Look at the ads on TV; what
do most appeal to? Go to the movies; how much sex is in most
movies today? Many of today's TV shows have crossed the line
and made sex one of the major hooks.

With all the sex that is being thrown at young people
today no wonder many believe that sex is love. Sex in and of
itself is not love. The physical without the other aspects of love
creates a void. Great sex is only great in the beginning. When
it becomes just something you do, it loses much of its magical
appeal.

I have had so many young ladies tell me "I wish I had
waited. I did it because it just seemed the thing to do. After
all, we were really close and it just seemed like the natural
next step. Boy, was I wrong. Once we had sex, the relationship
changed for the worst."

Sex without the other aspects of love creates emotional
confusion. There is such a difference between sex and romance.
Sex only sees the body and misses the person. Too many times
the *eros* expression of "I Love You" simply means *you have
something I want."*

Romance sees the person and expresses love as

150

spiritual, mental, emotional and physical. It sees the total person not simply the physical aspects of an individual.

Sex in and of itself can leave a person with a huge emotional void. It can create emotional scars that leave the person with an unhealthy view of love and sex.

The Greeks understood that so they gave us a second word for love — *philia*. Translated it means friendship. How important is friendship to a relationship?

Friendship is about respecting the other person. That means you would never do anything you know would hurt or damage the feelings they have for you.

Friendship is about trust. It is the feeling you can put your faith in this person. What they tell you, you can believe. This aspect of friendship removes the feelings of doubt and worry.

Friendship is about support. This involves knowing if you need them, they will be there. If there is an issue that needs to be talked through, you know they will be there and be willing to do what it takes to resolve the issue.

Friendship is about listening. This is about treating you as a person of value. It says, "what you have to say and add is of value, and I want to hear."

Yet, the Greeks knew you could feel *Eros* and not be "in love" with a person. The physical attraction might give you the feeling of "love," but on its own it couldn't take you to the feeling of "being in love."

They knew you could feel *philia* and not be "in love" with a person. The friendship is critical to growing the love between two people, but on its own it cannot create being "in love" with a person.

To take the meaning of "love" to a deeper and more

complete meaning the Greeks gave us the term *agape*. This is the only aspect of "love" that means *in love*. It is that aspect of love that takes the meaning of "love" to the deeper level of commitment.

Eros cannot create this feeling of complete commitment. Why? Because it only sees one aspect of the person — their physical presence. That limitation destroys the mature development of falling "in love" with a person. It is physical attraction that doesn't have the inner connections to take it deeper.

Philia cannot create this inner feeling of complete commitment. Yes, it is love, but it is based on the emotional connection between two people. That alone will not create the mature understandings you need to fall "in love."

Agape is the only level that allows two people to fall "in love" with each other. It is about loving the total person. Yes, it contains the physical; yes, it contains the friendship, but it doesn't stop there.

It contains the mental connection that is so important in walking together through the tough terrain that every relationship will face. How many times have you seen a couple lose the lustful feeling they had for each other. When the sex becomes commonplace, it loses the magic it contained. How many times have you seen the friendship weaken over a period of time? As each grows and are not growing together, the friendship weakens. No longer are they as close as they once were. No longer do they talk about all the little things they used to talk about. No longer do they share at the level they did in the beginning of the friendship.

There has to be a deeper aspect that takes you through the shifting sands of every relationship. As much as you would like to believe your marriage was made in heaven, there will always be the earthly aspects that keep it challenged. This shifting sand is where the relationship is tested. It is at these times the strength and commitment are put to the ultimate test. If there is only *eros* or *philia*, most relationships will not be able to handle the tremors that will be created. If there is agape, these times are seen as strengthening times. When *agape* is the foundation, the strength of the commitment will walk you through the times of challenge, fear and uncertainty.

Without *agape* as the foundation, there will not be the inner mental and emotional strength necessary to stay strong during the tremors. The strength of the foundation is what allows you to have the commitment. If the foundation is weak, the commitment to make it through will be weak. This is where most relationships falter. They lack the foundational strength; many assume that because they are married the strength of their love automatically grows. Nothing is further from the truth. The foundation takes continual work and shoring up. It doesn't stay strong because you are together. It stays strong because you are continuing to monitor and work on the areas that have weakened.

The most common areas of foundational weakening are:

- *You stop dating.*
- *Your relationship is driven by the needs of the children and you forget about the needs of the two of you.*
- *The communication grows weak because issues are not resolved.*
- *Building financial stability takes a higher priority than the emotional health of the two of you.*

153

Here are some questions for you to answer *honestly*:

- *Can you honestly say you are "in love" with your partner?*
- *Do you have a foundation that is strong when it comes to handling the tremors in your relationship?*
- *Are you wrestling with any of the things that weaken the foundation?*
- *Is your love relationship healthy?*

How Do You Stay In Love?
S *stay in truth, trust and respect*
T *take it at a manageable pace*
A *always continue to date each other*
Y *yearn for more love and growth*

WHAT ABOUT ME?

If there is no time for you, you will soon resent what others ask you to do for them.

Lynn put it this way. "I am so tired of being everyone's slave. I work, I take care of the kids, I wash, I clean, I take care of my husband and all I get is more demands. In the beginning I didn't mind, but now it is different. The kids are old enough to help around the house, but they don't. My husband comes home, sits in front of the TV, waits for me to fix dinner and then crawls into bed while I continue to do more housework. Richard, it just isn't fair. I am not their personal maid. I resent the way they treat me. I won't take it any more. I would love to just have some time for me."

Mary said it this way. "All I want is a little time for me. There has to be more to life than working and taking care of the family. Every time I think there is going to be some time for me, someone else needs something from me. I am so tired of being there for everyone. I want to have some time just for me. You have no idea how much I would love to run away and not tell anyone where I am."

Alice told me this. "I don't have a life. I used to, but not anymore. Everyone expects me to be there when they need me. I don't care if it is work, home, family or friends. They all expect me to drop everything and come running when they call. Well, they had better realize I am not going to be their slave. I need a life and they are taking it away from me. Not any more. I will not let them steal my life. They had better get used to the new selfish me. She is in control now."

Steal your life! Life is about purpose; it is about a plan for growth and development; it is about family and friends; it is

155

Others don't steal your time; you allow them to take it away from you.

about sharing yourself with those you love, *but* it is also about having time for you. All of us need time for self. Without it you become an empty shell filled with thoughts, ideas and dreams there never seem to be time for.

If you know me, you know my design for life. You live in a four-room house. The rooms are:

- BUSINESS ROOM
- FAMILY ROOM
- SOCIAL ROOM
- PERSONAL ROOM

Each of these rooms has a purpose in your life. Each is there to help bring purpose, calmness and clarity to the other rooms. They are there to support each other. When one room is out of sync with the others, there is confusion, lack of balance and a screaming for time in the other rooms.

Time is what most people are searching for. Most live at such an unmanageable pace, they never seem to be in control of their life. Most are spread so thin; they get exhausted just thinking about all they need to do. Most see stacks no matter where they look. That is only good for so long. Then, at some point they find themselves feeling angry over all the expectations that surround their life. They feel pressured; they feel they will never get caught up; they feel there will never be time for self. They feel trapped! When that feeling of being trapped sets in, you no longer have a life. What you have is an existence.

Brad was my seatmate on a flight from Dallas to Ontario. I was reading <u>Golf Digest</u> when he interrupted me. "Do you play golf?"

I paused my reading and responded, "Yes! Golf is my passion. Any day I am not on the road you can find me on a golf course."

"I really love the game."

"Do you play much?"

"I used to. I used to play two or three times a week. Then, things changed. I got promoted into management and the demands on my time really changed. Following that, we had our first child and recently, our second child. There is no time for golf. All I do is work and spend time with the family."

There was a long pause as he stared out the window. Then, he looked back at me and continued, "We even live on a golf course. It is tough watching all those people go by. I have to admit I am jealous. I love the game so much, but for now there is no time. I'll get back to it in a few years. Someday I'll get my life back, but for now many of the things I want for me have to be put on hold."

There was another pause, another moment of reflection as he stared out the window and then these words. "Don't get me wrong. I love my life, but I wish there was more time for me. I know it will come, but I wish I could see it happening soon. Know what? When there is no time for you, you find yourself questioning all the things you've done that have taken your time away."

The look on his face told me it was and it wasn't okay. *Someday I'll get back to having a life!* There are so many that live hoping someday they will have a life. The issue is not as much about time as it is about the control of time.

Have you ever resented the fact there was no time for you? Have you ever reached the point you got upset when you were asked to do something that cut into the time you had planned for you?

So many spend their life with the anticipation that

158

someday they will have a life. They work — *many times at jobs they don't enjoy.* They go home — *many times to a relationship that is not growing or fulfilling.* They eat, sleep and get up and face another day where they give their time to everyone except their self. Over a period of time this design takes a toll on them. Over a period of time the wearing on them begins to affect the relationships they have with the others in their life. The result is the loss of the quality connection with those they share time and space. Soon, the lack of personal time creates a sense of resentment toward those who share their life.

Resentment is such an interesting emotion. Rather than seeking to understand what is happening, you find yourself emotionally reacting to what you're facing. The emotional reaction causes you to speed up, and the speeding up creates a bigger reaction.

Time is something you work to protect; yet, it is a constant challenge to control. Everywhere you turn someone is wanting some of your time. You can handle the expectations as long as there is some time left for you. When there is no time for you, the resentment grows.

Have you been there? Have you ever felt this serge of resentment race through you? The request doesn't have to be anything major. It can be very simple, but the fact it is taking *your* time sends this serge of resentment through you.

It sounds simple to say *if they are stealing your personal time, just tell them no!* As simple as it sounds, most people cannot say "no."

Sandy is one of those people who cannot say "no" to anyone. She approached me after my program on <u>Balancing The Rooms of Your Life</u>. During the program, I made the

159

statement *if you want time for yourself, you have to master three words. They are "no," "delegate" and "organization."*

As she approached, the look on her face was one of confusion. I looked at her and said, "I think you have a question for me."

"Yes, I think I have more than one."

"Okay, ask me."

"I understand what you are saying, but it is not as simple as you make it sound. You said I had to master the word *no*. I know there is wisdom in what you are saying, but it is not easy to look at people who are dependent on you and tell them *no*."

The pause told me she was wrestling with how to say what she was feeling. I looked at her and said, "I bet you feel guilty just thinking about using that word."

"Yea," she responded with this look of understanding on her face. "That's what I was struggling to put into words. Sure I could tell people *no*, but I would feel guilty. Yet, when I do everything for them, and there is no time left for me I get angry at them. Strange, don't you think?"

"Not really. Guilt creates confusion. You have this feeling of what you want to do, but because of your need to be liked or your need to be needed, you cannot do what will grant you personal freedom."

I paused to let her mentally catch up. "Sandy, do you understand that personal freedom is about having control of your life? Do you understand that freedom is about having time for you? When everyone takes your time and you are left with none for you, the natural result is feeling angry, which turns around and feeds the guilt you are feeling. It is a vicious circle of emotional drain. What you have to do is get over the feeling of guilt. What you have to do is make yourself a priority in your life. Others will treat you in the manner you tell them is okay. You were not created to be anyone's slave. You were created for happiness, personal fulfillment and freedom. You will not have those as long as you are sacrificing yourself in order to take care of others. One other thing you need to understand: *As your resentment grows, so does the quality of your presence.* When you resent what you are doing, you simply go through the motions. That will drain you even more, and that will feed your resentment. Does this make sense to you?"

"Yes, it makes a lot of sense. I just don't know if I can do it. Maybe I wasn't meant to have a life."

"Sandy, everyone was meant to have a life. Your life is yours to design. Others don't steal your time; you allow them to take it away from you."

I haven't heard from her since that conversation. My gut tells me she is still a person in need of a life. A life that is going to happen someday is a life that most likely will not happen. If there is no time for you, you will resent the life you have. It really is not as much about having time as it is taking control of your time. That is your choice.

Here are some questions for you to answer *honestly*:

- *Do you resent what others ask of you?*
- *Are you good at saying "no"?*
- *Do you manage your life or does it manage you?*

How Do You Learn To Have Time For You?

T *take control; don't give it away*
I *insist on having the personal time*
M *make yourself a priority in your life*
E *emotionally master the word "no"*

CONCLUSION
Relationships don't grow on their own;
they take time, commitment, desire and
constant maintenance.

Here is the tragedy I see. Most relationships are not growing; they are existing. They are not improving; they are being tolerated.

Do you understand how sad that is? Two people come together to build a life together. They have this special feeling for each other. That special feeling is identified as "love." That special feeling is seen as self-sufficient. In reality, it is a very insecure emotion. On many days, it is being challenged through events that are not confronted, behavior that contradicts words and the loss of feeling special to the other person.

Yes, relationships are going to stumble. Yes, relationships are going to go through troubled waters. Yes, human beings are going to have conflict. Yes, love is going to rise and fall. Yes, there are going to be moments of disappointment. Yes, there are going to be moments of doubt, but no, this does not have to destroy the relationship.

It is about putting the building blocks in place. It is about strengthening your commitment. It is about facing issues head on that can tear the relationship apart. It is about each person in the relationship committing to their personal growth. It is learning to blend, rather than working to change the other person.

It is all about continuing to fall "in love," rather than "falling out of love." That means working together, not pulling apart. It means striving to build the relationship from the inside out. It means laying a foundation of behavior that pushes the

163

relationship to the next dimension, rather than sitting around and staring at what is wrong with the way things are.

Stumbling blocks are the result of people not paying attention to people. Building Blocks are the result of people committing to people and living up to their commitment.

Staying In Love Demands:
D *desire that blossoms into love*
E *emotional togetherness*
M *managing the tough times*
A *affection in public; romance in private*
N *not letting silence rule*
D *dedication to growing the relationship*
S *self-improvement*

Share It With Others

To order copies of this book,
Call 1-800-368-8255
or (757) 873-7722
or visit
www.RichardFlint.com

Special quantity discounts are available
for bulk purchases.

Please allow 2-3 weeks for US delivery.
Canada & International orders
please allow 4-6 weeks for delivery.

<u>Other Books by Richard Flint, CSP:</u>

Building Blocks *For Strengthening Your Life*

Building Blocks *For Strengthening Your Relationships*

Building Blocks *For Improving Customer Relationships*

Building Blocks *For Controlling Stress*

Breaking Free

Life Is A Maze

Quiet Please

Feelings

It Takes A Lot Of Pain To Grow Up

Reflections

Sometimes I Really Need To Cry